SO-AXJ-907

PRESCHOOL
BRUNSWICK RECREATION COMMISSION
Our Goal: "Recreation For Everybody"
BRUNSWICK RECREATION CENTER
FEDERAL STREET, BRUNSWICK, MAINE

your
FIVE-YEAR-
OLD

your FIVE-YEAR-OLD
Sunny and Serene

by Louise Bates Ames
and Frances L. Ilg

Gesell Institute of Child Development

*Illustrated with photographs
by Betty David*

DELACORTE PRESS/NEW YORK

Published by
Delacorte Press
1 Dag Hammarskjold Plaza
New York, New York 10017

Copyright © 1979 by The Gesell Institute of Child Development,
Louise Bates Ames and Frances L. Ilg

Manufactured in the United States of America

First printing

Designed by Giorgetta Bell McRee

LIBRARY OF CONGRESS CATALOGING IN PUBLICATION DATA

Ames, Louise Bates.
Your five-year-old.

Bibliography: p.
Includes index.
1. Child development.   I. Ilg, Frances Lillian,
1902-   joint author.   II. Gesell Institute of
Child Development, New Haven.   III. Title.
HQ772.A474   155.4'23   78-11622
ISBN 0-440-09876-9

To our daughters,
Joan and Tordis,

and our grandchildren,
Carol, Clifford, Douglas, Karl, Mark,
Tommy, and Whittier

CONTENTS

FOREWORD

Norms, or descriptions, of what a parent may expect his or her child to do at any given age make some people feel secure. They make other people anxious or even angry. But we have found that most parents do seem to find it comforting to know more or less what they may expect of their child at any given age.

Many find it especially comforting when their child is going through a difficult or demanding stage to learn that it is all very "normal"—that other children behave in these ways too.

We ourselves have been studying child behavior for the past forty years or more and our own studies were preceded by those of Dr. Arnold Gesell, the Director of our former Clinic at Yale, in whose honor our present Institute was founded.

All these studies, which have involved literally thousands of boys and girls, have convinced us that human behavior develops in a highly patterned way. It seems quite possible to describe rather clearly the more or less predictable stages through which any kind of behavior— motor, language, adaptive, personal-social—develops.

We can tell you with high confidence what the stages of development will be in the more or less *average* boy or girl.

But of course hardly anybody is truly "average." As we

shall describe in rather great detail in Chapter Nine of this book, *every child is an individual, different in many ways from every other child living—even from his or her own identical twin.*

So when we tell you that Four is wild and wonderful, Five is calm and serene, Six something else again, this does not mean that *all* children at any one of these ages will behave or should behave just exactly in the ways we describe.

Some perfectly normal boys and girls will be ahead of our schedule. Some will be behind, and then, of course, there are those who will hit it right on the nose. And it is certainly not a cause for concern in any case.

Not only will there be many differences in timing, but also in level of equilibrium or disequilibrium. Some children, at all ages, are charmingly well adjusted, easy to live with. Others, no matter how skillful and caring their parents, may be difficult at any stage of childhood, or at all.

Some children seem to develop in a fairly integrated way. All the different kinds of behavior occur rather evenly. So they will be right at, or above, or below their age in motor, adaptive, language, and what we call personal-social behavior. Others may be way ahead of customary expectations in their talking but below age in motor ways. Or just the opposite.

We have described the kinds of individual differences we expect later in this book. But so that no reader will be made anxious by what we say, let us emphasize right here at the very beginning that *the descriptions of expected behaviors which we give are only averages,* generalizations, ways that many of the children we see do conduct themselves.

We have sometimes likened the descriptions we give in this and other similar books to a map of a country through which you may plan to travel. We *can* tell you what the country is like. We *cannot* tell you what your trip will be like. You may go faster or slower than the usual traveler. You may take more side excursions than the average. You may even at times backtrack. The map does not guarantee what you will do or even tell you what you *ought* to do. It merely defines the territory.

Most people find maps quite useful. Many parents find our maps of the terrain of child behavior useful, too. So use our maps if you like and we hope that you will find, as do many, that they provide helpful orientation. Please do *not* use them for comparing your own child with our hypothetical average and then making adverse judgments either about our norms *or* about your child. Each child is a wonderfully unique and special person. We hope only to help you appreciate him more as he passes through his various stages of development.

chapter one
CHARACTERISTICS OF AGE FIVE

What can you as a parent expect of your Five-year-old boy or girl? It is a pleasure to tell you that with most Five-year-olds, some very good times are ahead. Five wants to be good, means to be good, and more often than not succeeds in being good.

Perhaps most delightful of all his characteristics is that he enjoys life so much and looks so consistently on its sunny side. "Today is my lucky day," he will tell you as he jumps out of bed in the morning. Or, enthusiastically, "Today I'm going to do all the good things and none of the bad things." Or even more comprehensively, "I want to be good all the time and not do any of the bad things. I'll do whatever you say and I won't make a fuss."

In his determination to do everything *just right,* he may ask permission for even the simplest thing and will then beam with pleasure when his mother smiles and says, "Yes, you may have an apple, dear."

Even his language is on the positive side: "Sure!" "All right!" "Fine!" "Lovely," "Wonderful" are among his favorite words, and "I just love ———" is a constant refrain.

In fact, there are those mothers who worry that perhaps their Five-year-old is "almost too good," as they put it. Our reassurance to such mothers is that they need not worry. Such goodness cannot last forever. If it did the child would

be too compliant to stand up for his rights in what, for any growing child, will be an increasingly challenging world.

The key to all this goodness may be that for a few months at least, Mother is the center of the child's world. He not only wants to please her, he wants to be near her. Wants to talk with her, play with her, help her with her housework, follow her around the house. Many Fives would actually rather stay in the house with Mother than go out to play with their friends.

Such adoration and acceptance, after the somewhat stormy days of Four, are certainly restful and welcomed by any mother, especially if she has more than one child. Five's adoration of his parents is unquestionably heart-warming.

But Five's positiveness and acceptance of the world extends even beyond his parents. As one little girl expressed it, "I love everybody in the whole wide world. Even God." Another, when she heard the song "He's Got the Whole World in His Hands," explained, "It would have to be God. Nobody else could do that."

Five as a rule lives very closely in the here and now, and he cares very much about his own room, his own home, his street, neighborhood, and kindergarten room. He is not particularly interested in the new and strange and usually does not seek adventure for its own sake. The typical Four-year-old has been described by us as "wild and wonderful." Wonderful he may be at times, but his wildness can get him into trouble.

Not so with Five. He is by nature quieter, more pulled in, closer to home. He not only prefers to stay within prescribed boundaries but feels most comfortable with the tried and true. The time that interests him is now; the place he likes best, here.

One of the important keys in understanding the remarkable smoothness of a Five-year-old is that he has an almost uncanny ability to judge what he can and cannot do. That is, he is self-limiting. With tremendous accuracy he judges what things are and what are not within his ability, and he tries only what he is sure of. His success then builds self-confidence. He isn't smug, but he is secure. This means that he uses much less energy than earlier in resisting others in order to prove to himself that he is his own boss.

Unlike the child of some other ages, Five often shows a remarkable ability to protect himself from overstimulation. As one little girl said while visiting friends of her parents', "I can't go to see your friends every night or I might get dizzy." Another, while a visitor at nursery school not her own, told her mother on the second day, "I'm a little shy in this new school and it makes me feel a little funny in my stomach. But I think if you'll stay for just a few minutes I'll feel all right."

4

Five is usually not a worrier. Six will worry that Mother may not be there when he comes home from school. Five assumes that she will be there, not only now but forever. The average child of this age seems to take for granted that he and his parents are eternal. He does not delve too far into the past (even though with his good memory he can remember things that happened to him when he was younger), and gives relatively little thought to the future. He likes life the way it is, is satisfied with himself, and adores his parents. Though not given to excess, he can sometimes be caught boasting about both mother and father and quoting them as the *ultimate* authorities.

There is also now a strong feeling for family. A child may tell the family cat, "This belonged to the whole family even before you were born."

To the adult, a Five-year-old is tremendously appealing with his serious air. He is impressed with his own increasing ability to take little responsibilities and to imitate grown-up behavior. He is very proud when parent or teacher compliments him on something he has done. "Just like a grown-up," he may exclaim proudly after some mature activity. Or it may be just his own age that impresses him: "I can do that because Five-year-olds can tie."

Though the typical Five-year-old is not particularly expansive in most ways, he *is* expansive intellectually. He loves to be read to, loves to be talked to, loves to learn new facts. He likes to practice his own intellectual abilities— to show his mother how he can print his name, or write the numbers up to five, or spell out some of the words in his favorite books.

All things considered, the age of Five, for most children, can truthfully be called a golden age!

FIVE-AND-A-HALF TO SIX

So here you are, sailing along, happy as a lark. Your little son or daughter for almost six unbelievable months may have been good as gold. He or she not only plans to be good and wants to be good but actually *is* good. This age can be a parent's dream come true.

Thus it can be more than a little disconcerting when all of a sudden things aren't so rosy any more. That little angel who responded, oh, so easily, with "Yes, I will," now is quite likely to say "No, I won't."

That child for whom mother was indeed the center of the world begins to show every evidence that he is now reserving that spot for himself. What's gotten into him?

Quite possibly, no more than the beginnings of Six-year-oldness, a time that often brings trouble into the calmest households. Not yet a full-fledged Six, nevertheless the child of Five-and-a-half shows an all-too-great readiness to disobey, to go against what is asked or expected of him. And he doesn't always do this gently. "Brash" and "combative" are adjectives that mothers use in describing this child, and all with good reason.

Five-and-a-half is characteristically hesitant, dawdling, indecisive, or, at the opposite extreme, overdemanding and explosive. Behavior is all too often characterized by the opposite extreme, which we saw earlier at Two-and-a-half years of age. That is, the child may be extremely shy one minute and then extremely bold the next; very affectionate, and then almost without warning very antagonistic.

And when he doesn't have the courage to defy you outright, he dawdles—which amounts to almost the same thing. That is, whatever you want him to do, very often does not get done.

Emotionally the child of this age may seem to be in an almost constant state of tension, though fortunately most are calmer at school than at home. The child finds it hard to conclude an explosion or sulk or burst of tears once it has begun. This may be the beginning, once again, of a tantrum age.

Physically, too, we see signs of a breakup. The almost predictably healthy Five-year-old now suddenly has many colds, headaches, earaches, stomachaches. Or his feet hurt, his face hurts. He may even revert to toileting acci-

dents when he is overexcited. And physically rather placid Five now has come to a place where there is an increase of tensional outlets—many hand-to-mouth gestures; chewing on loose clothing, biting or tapping a pencil.

Motorwise there is more restlessness, less composure

than we saw at Five. Pencil grasp may be awkward and there may be frequent change of grasp. Though he may not, as at Six, "trip over a piece of string," his total body seems less under his control than just formerly. And it becomes increasingly difficult for him to sit still for long periods.

Visually boys and girls are much more experimental than six months earlier. The simple, sure reality of Five is breaking up. Thus the child frequently loses his visual orientation and may often reverse his numbers or letters. (This is one of the several reasons why we feel this is not a good age to teach reading or writing. It is just too confusing for the child to work with words and letters when he is already having trouble figuring out the order of things.)

Eyes and hands now function with less speed and sureness than they did at Five, though behavior is gathering content and flow. The child at this age may know when he doesn't *have* the right answer; he just doesn't know how to *get* it. But he does recognize inconsistencies. His organization is breaking up, his reality often shattered. And in a way he enjoys this. Thus the child of this age may voluntarily and experimentally cross his eyes when he doesn't understand something, when he is surprised, or when he wants to be silly.

Even the child's *teeth* are breaking up, so to speak. One by one those pearly, even baby teeth are starting to go, beginning with the lower central incisors, which may merely loosen or may actually fall out.

As most parents know, few stages of perfection last forever. So though it may be disappointing, it should in no way be surprising that the golden age of Five gives way in time to the complexity and confusion of Five-and-a-half to Six.

Even in infancy, rather predictable stages of equilibrium alternate with stages of disequilibrium; stages of inwardizing alternate with ages of expansion. Figure 1 illustrates what a parent may expect in the early years from eighteen months through Six-and-a-half. Five, as

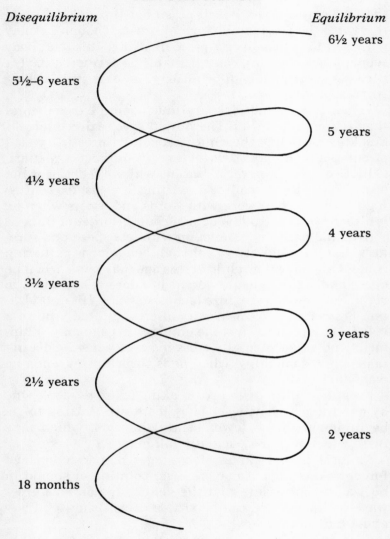

Disequilibrium   *Equilibrium*

6½ years

5½–6 years

5 years

4½ years

4 years

3½ years

3 years

2½ years

2 years

18 months

Figure 1

Alternation of Ages of Equilibrium and Disequilibrium

you will see clearly, is on the side of equilibrium, an equilibrium that in some children does not break up until Six. But in others, disequilibrium and difficulty may start as early as Five-and-a-half. Don't be discouraged when it does; don't feel that something is wrong with either your child or your handling of him or her.

Breakup of any early smooth stage must come before the child can attain a higher and more mature stage of equilibrium. But that higher stage will come, you can be almost certain.

WARNING!

We'd like to offer an important word of advice for all parents, regardless of the age of their child. *Do not take too seriously what anybody tells you (and that includes us) about how your child will behave.*

Child behavior, for all reasonably normal children, does develop in a patterned way. Stages of equilibrium are followed by stages of disequilibrium before the child can reach some succeeding stage of equilibrium. That this will happen, we are reasonably sure. And we can tell you approximately when these things will happen in the usual course of development.

What we cannot tell you is exactly when they will occur in your own individual child. Nor can we tell the extent to which either breakup or adjustment will go. Some children seem always to live a bit on the side of disequilibrium. Even at calm ages or stages they have trouble with themselves and those around them.

Other children, even in the same family, may always seem to live on the brighter side of life. Living is easy for them; people and things do what they expect. It is easy for them to be good.

So what we try to do is tell you about behavior that is frequently characteristic of the different ages, not so that you will worry but so that you can know what to expect and then *not* worry when your own child's behavior is less than what you'd like it to be.

chapter two
THE CHILD AND OTHERS

It should be quite obvious from the preceding chapter that person number one in the life of any Five-year-old is his mother. He loves her best. He wants to please her most. "My own best mummy" is what he often calls her.

Fives, in spite of all their apparent confidence, do need quite a bit of reassurance from mother. They like her to tell them, and frequently, how much she loves them. So, though they can affirm "I like you and you like me," they still often question, "Do you love me?"

What Mother says is as good as law to them. One kindergartner we know, when criticized by his teacher, replied calmly, "I'm not a bad boy. I'm a good boy. My Mummy says I'm a good boy." It is very important to him that his mother should make such a statement.

Fives feel so close to their mothers that they sometimes overestimate her ability to read their minds. They are often quick and a little impatient and don't always give all the necessary clues as to what they are talking about. Then they tend to be quite angry if she doesn't pick up on their story at once. It takes a quick wit to be a mother.

And, admittedly, as they move on toward Five-and-a-half, if things go wrong, children will sometimes take things out on mother. So, when Beth's mother came to pick her up one day at kindergarten, Beth greeted her not with her usual shout of joy but with a frown and the proclamation, "I don't like you."

Mother, wisely, asked her daughter calmly, "What happened?" "There was a birthday party and all the other girls wore dresses and you made me wear my overalls," Beth replied.

The fact that Five adores his mother by no means implies that Father is out in the cold. Most Fives are very fond of their fathers, proud of them, and love their company. Fathers do not as a rule receive as much affection from their children but, on the other hand, if the child does have an outburst of temper, it is more likely to be against his mother than his father. And in the insecurity of the night, it is Mother whom he wants most.

(It is altogether possible that in a one-parent family in which Father is doing all the parenting, a Five-year-old would be as devoted to his father as he ordinarily is to Mother, but we have no data to support this.)

Grandparents are extremely important to the Five-year-old. We know from experience how warm and responsive the relationship can be. However, when you ask a Five-year-old about his or her grandparents, he often sounds as if he is more interested in what they give him than in how they feel about him. So, when asked what the best thing about their grandmother is, Fives often say, "She makes us good food and gives us things." Of their grandfather, they say, "He loves us and gives us nice presents." The best thing about visiting grandparents is that "They give us things and make us good food."

Interestingly enough, their descriptions of grandparents are chiefly in terms of hair: "Gray and curly," "Kind of white," "She has four wigs," "Not much hair, kinda bald."

Specific other comments include: "She's nice, gives us candy"; "They're nice to me"; "They take me to get ice cream"; "Gives us lots of presents"; "Lets us stay up late"; "They're nice—I like them"; "Nice—gives me good presents at Christmas"; "They treat me nice."

A Five-year-old's relationship to his siblings is apt to

improve somewhat now. Many Fives play reasonably well with older siblings and tend to be extremely kind and protective to those who are younger. Some girls are regular little mothers to their younger siblings and especially to any baby in the family. It is important to appreciate that their instinct for mothering may exceed their ability to take responsibility. So, a Five-year-old needs to be supervised when holding or caring for a baby.

Five often gets on best with children outside his immediate family, especially children his own age. With his natural desire to please and to have things go smoothly, he is a much easier playmate than he was at Four or than he may be at Six. But even a Five-year-old can have trouble at times, and two children tend to play together better than do three.

With older children, the Five-year-old may be quite docile and may for instance even be willing to play the role of baby when children are playing house.

However, even the friendly Five-year-old sometimes runs into a child with whom he just cannot get along. Whose fault this is is not the question. Since Five, with his gentleness and good will, tends to be quite vulnerable socially, he should be protected from the company of an overaggressive or incompatible child.

With strangers or when visiting, a Five-year-old can be a polite and friendly little person. If he is not tired it can be a real pleasure to have him along. In many cases his manners and his stamina are now adequate so that he is no longer a menace on a train or plane, in a restaurant or downtown shopping. If plans are made with his tender age in mind, it can often be more fun to have him with you than not.

And now how about that important new person in his life, his kindergarten teacher? Of course, nowadays many children have already had a nursery-school experience by Five, and in many instances teacher is respected and loved next only to the child's parents themselves.

A kindergarten teacher is in a slightly different position from a nursery-school teacher. No matter how loosely the schoolroom is run, there *are* more demands on the child now. Fortunately, most Fives are quite up to the demands made, and most Five-year-olds like their teacher. The relationship tends to be matter-of-fact and friendly. With his customary docility, the ordinary kindergartner obeys his teacher as a matter of course and outside of school quotes her as an authority.

The child usually likes his teacher very much, but the relationship tends to be less intimate than it was when he was in nursery school, or than it will be later. He does depend on her, when he wants something or for attention, but he sometimes complains at home, "The teacher makes me do things." In general, however, the relationship is a pleasant one. If it is not going well, often having the teacher visit the child's home helps out a lot. Parents should realize how much this could mean to the child. The visit doesn't have to be long or formal. We have seen a child's whole attitude toward school and his teacher improve after even one short visit.

chapter three
ROUTINES, HEALTH, AND TENSIONAL OUTLETS

By the time a child is Five, one might suppose that he should know how to eat. And of course he does, as far as actually getting food into himself goes. But if a household has exacting standards, the child of this age may still fall short. He dawdles, talks too much, may even toward the end of a meal ask to be fed. He wriggles in his chair, though he doesn't as a rule have to leave the table to go to the bathroom as he did at Four. And most do not fall out of their chairs as they may at Six.

Appetite has usually improved. In fact it is usually quite adequate, though some meals may be better than others. Not all eat three "good" meals a day. But with their interest in finishing things, their normal perseverance, and their wish to do what other people want them to, Fives often manage to clean up their plates, even though it may seem to you as if it is taking forever.

Food preferences are still rather marked. Five likes plain, simple cooking, and may thus like best meat, potatoes, a raw vegetable, milk, and fruit. Gravies, casseroles, puddings, cooked root vegetables, anything complicated or with a strong taste, may be refused. The child especially dislikes stringy and lumpy foods. But some-

18

times when a Five-year-old is at a restaurant or visiting he will eat foods that he would normally refuse at home.

Most Fives need little help, unless they are tired or it is the end of a long meal. Most can use a knife for spreading even though they are not yet ready to cut their meat.

Five's table manners are not yet too polished, but fortunately many parents still do not expect as much as they may in another year. So, often a meal with the whole family can go quite happily. Five still does tend to talk too much and also to talk with his mouth full. There is some spilling. Some at this age will still wear a bib though most prefer a napkin tucked in at the neck. But in general, mealtimes go reasonably well. Five really likes to do what is expected of him, at the table as well as everywhere else.

More and more parents are becoming aware of the importance of serving good, wholesome, well-balanced meals. Increasingly, especially since the writings of Dr. Ben Feingold,[1] people are realizing that a poor diet and particularly the intake of artificial colorings and flavorings in food, drink, and even medicine may have a very bad effect on the behavior of some children. Feingold believes that much of the so-called hyperactivity, which is on the increase these days, is due to an improper diet.

Dr. Ray C. Wunderlich[2] emphasizes that many more children than most realize are allergic to certain foods and that much undesirable behavior, both at home and at school, is caused by undetected allergies to food and drink.

And Dr. Lendon Smith[3] in his excellent book, *Improving Your Child's Behavior Chemistry,* points out that many children behave badly because their bodies don't work right—don't work right because their owners' brains just don't get proper nourishment.

He tells us that if the cortex, or forebrain, isn't properly nourished, the animal, or emotional, brain takes over. Thus, with nothing to stop him, the poorly nourished child often becomes violent and aggressive.

Unfortunately, the proper functioning of the forebrain

depends on constant nourishment, since it cannot store nourishment. Improper diet, especially the consumption of too much white flour and sugar, can interfere with the body's functions. Too much sugar, for instance, *lowers* the blood sugar in the body to the extent that the forebrain does not function. Thus the Dr. Jekyll/Mr. Hyde child who is so good one minute and so dreadful the next may actually be suffering from a malnourished forebrain.

Smith especially recommends, along with cutting down on white flour and sugar, the eating of plenty of protein—nuts, cheese, tuna fish, and peanut butter.

SLEEPING

Bedtime, as the child moves out of the preschool years, becomes increasingly easy for most children. Bedtime is usually somewhere between 7 and 8 o'clock and most go to bed rather willingly. They often like to have stories read to them, either in the living room or after they reach their own room.

Getting ready for bed usually goes smoothly. Many continue to take a toy animal or special blanket to bed with them. If they don't go to sleep quickly, some like to "read" to themselves. Still others like to lie quietly in the dark, singing or talking to themselves.

A few still need to get up frequently for a drink, something to eat, or to go to the bathroom, but most Five-year-olds can now take care of their own needs without bothering their parents.

So far, all's well. But the Five-year-old is a good example of what we describe as *good days, bad nights.* So, the typical Five-year-old who often has been so good all day is somewhat unfairly rewarded by nightmares and bad dreams at night. Frightening animal dreams predominate and the child may awaken crying or screaming.

At first it can be extremely disconcerting to have the child whom you put to bed so happy cry out in terror a few hours later, tears coursing down his cheeks, and maybe even striking out against your comforting hand. Usually it is hard for the child to tell much about what he dreamed, but fortunately most can be comforted rather quickly with some hugging and reassuring conversation. Such dreams, frightening or not, are fairly common at this age and are rarely a matter for great concern.

Occasionally, fear may even invade the daytime hours and your child will tell you, looking rather sheepish and surprised at himself, "I'm afraid." Sometimes this needs to be talked out, but often a change of subject or activity works just as well.

The average Five-year-old tends to wake up between 7 and 8 A.M. after an eleven-hour sleep. Most of them can take care of themselves. That is, they can close the window, put on their bathrobe and slippers, go to the bathroom, and then occupy themselves by coloring in bed or looking at books until it is time to get up.

In spite of occasional nightmares, Five's sleep behavior is usually pleasant and easy.

ELIMINATION

Though many children are very good about toileting routines even at Four, some still do need reminding and also are quite likely to report on what they have done, after they come out of the bathroom.

Not so at Five. Most Five-year-olds have their toileting very well in control. Most now take all or nearly all of the responsibility for this function themselves.

They urinate infrequently, so they don't seem to have it on their minds. This may result in their putting off going to the bathroom when they actually need to go. Wriggling and hopping on one foot are clues to the adult that the child needs to be reminded.

As at Four, some find it hard to interrupt their play outside to go to the bathroom. If accidents tend to occur, a wise mother might remind the child that after a certain interval she will ring a bell or blow a whistle, and that will be his signal to come in for a quick trip to the bathroom. And a child may also need to be reminded to "go" before a trip or outing.

We have no exact figures on bed-wetting at night. Possibly half the children can stay dry all night or with a pick-up at the time parents go to bed. If a child is already wet at that time, and also is wet in the morning, it's quite obvious that the pick-up has served little purpose except that he or she won't be quite so wet in the morning.

If parents prefer to pick their child up for night toileting, it is our preference *not* to wake him entirely. This provides less of an interruption, and he is likely to get back to sleep more quickly.

At any rate, if your Five-year-old still is wetting at night, our advice is just to pad him up carefully and provide a rubber sheet to protect the mattress.

We do not personally consider bed-wetting at night, at Five, a problem, except from a practical point of view. There are conditioning devices that desperate parents can use, although ideally these should be used only under the guidance of a pediatrician and not started before Six at the earliest. Among those we like best are two called U-Trol, distributed by J. G. Shuman Associates, Box 306, Scotch Plains, New Jersey 07076; and Dry-O-Matic, distributed by Dry-O-Matic Company, 610 Allcott, Marshall, Michigan 49068. Either can be bought for under fifty dollars.

Bowel movements in most Fives are usually down to a routine and cause little difficulty for either parent or child. Some children have a rather definite time of day when they perform this function; with others it may be any old time. Most, but not all, have a bowel movement every day. Occasionally prune juice or some mild laxative may be needed.

As with urination, there is much less reporting to Mother about what the child has accomplished than there was at Four. This is restful for everybody.

The few boys who still resisted training by the tiresome habit of dirtying their pants are even fewer now (though this may return at Six in some). It is fair to say that it is the unusual Five who has this problem.

BATH AND DRESSING

Bath: The typical Five-year-old is pretty good about washing his hands before meals, especially if reminded. That is, he does not as a rule think of it himself; on the other hand, he makes no major objection and even does a pretty good job.

A total bath is something else again. He likes his bath and will participate as much as he can, but his abilities are limited. As Dr. Arnold Gesell, the original Director of our Clinic, once put it, "Children of this age still need some assistance in the niceties of cleanliness, neatness and manicuring." To say the least!

In fact, the child may be best at cleaning his hands and knees, and he will probably need quite a bit of help with other parts of his body. He may get stuck on one knee, washing it over and over and needing encouragement to shift even to his second knee. Of course, mother still needs to draw the bath water.

So it cannot be said that Five is an accomplished bather, but he *is* cooperative and enthusiastic, and bath for many can be a pleasant, relaxing occasion. But in the interests of saving time, many mothers prefer to do the bathing themselves. Some Fives still like to play with their toys while being bathed but many have given this up.

Dressing: Mothers of Five-year-olds tend to report, "He can but he doesn't." That is, he has most of the abilities needed, except for tying shoelaces or buttoning difficult buttons, but he often fails to use even the abilities he has.

Some mothers find that it helps if clothes are laid out singly, in the right order, on the floor. Otherwise the child is apt to get them on backward.

How much help the mother gives depends, of course, on how skillful the child is, and some Fives do take on quite a bit of responsibility. Some are able to choose two or three days of the week when they will be (mostly) responsible for dressing themselves, or at least for doing most of the dressing. Others really prefer to leave much of it up to Mother.

Undressing is still easier than dressing.

Regardless of how much responsibility they themselves show about getting garments on and off, few take very good care of their clothes. Even those girls who are clothes-conscious and want to look nice do not yet take good care of their dresses.

TENSIONAL OUTLETS

Five is not a particularly tense age, and so it comes as no surprise that the average Five-year-old exhibits relatively few tensional outlets as compared with his younger self.

There are now fewer facial grimaces, though a nose may twitch or an eye may blink. More likely there are separate hand-to-face gestures, nose picking, nail biting, or perhaps most usually, thumb sucking.

Though many children do give up sucking their thumbs by the time they are Five, in others this behavior persists. It occurs especially with fatigue or when the child is getting ready for sleep. It also sometimes occurs when the child is watching television or being read to. If this behavior seems persistent and needed, many parents permit it.

In other cases, when the behavior seems to be weakening and if the parent is very tired of it, giving it up can sometimes be induced by covering the thumb with a Band-aid or removing the accessory blanket or other object that the child customarily uses as he sucks. However, as Kathryn Ernst's *Danny and His Thumb* suggests, many parents today are more concerned with making a thumb-sucking child feel all right about his sucking than in getting him to give it up.

Earlier tensional outlets such as rocking and head banging have largely been given up by now, and Five is not a big age for temper tantrums.

In a behavior examination situation, tensional outlet is chiefly verbal, rather than emotional or motor as earlier. In school, if the child is tense, his hand goes briefly to various parts of head or body. He may grasp his thighs or scratch an arm or leg, or pull at his clothes. Or he may lift his buttocks from his chair without actually rising.

Masturbation seems to be a quite individual matter. We have never observed it to the extent that others report, though we share the general feeling that it is harmless. Many parents, when they notice a child masturbating, simply tell him that if he is going to do this, it's better to do it in private.

By Five-and-a-half and as the child moves on toward the more anxious age of Six, tensional outlets are likely to increase both in number and severity. And now one child may show several different types of overflow behavior. Hand-to-mouth gestures, nose picking, nail biting, thumb sucking may increase, and in some there is a great deal of throat clearing. Others smack their lips and click with their tongues. If school is difficult or demanding, stuttering, nail biting, and thumb sucking may become quite conspicuous. And in school, the child is apt to chew, bite, or tap his pencil. Girls especially may chew on their hair.

HEALTH

For the most part, assuming that your child is of a relatively healthy temperament, his health at this age will be pretty good, except for the communicable diseases he or she may catch. Whooping cough and chicken pox take the lead. Measles, once very prevalent, is now under better control.

Some Fives have only one or two colds a winter in contrast to their greater prevalence at Four and especially at Six. Stomachaches, which are fairly common, may be related to either the too-speedy intake of food or to the need to have a bowel movement, a need that may have been put off too long.

chapter four
DISCIPLINE

Now, how about those so-called techniques that parents find so useful in getting their children to do what they want them to do? "Tricks," some grandparents call them and feel that they are deceitful. As they remember it, they had such good control over their own children that they never had to resort to such measures.

Tricks or not, there are many ages, especially Two-and-a-half, Three-and-a-half, and Four, when many parents find that a good technique can be a lifesaver.

But there are a few gentle, compliant ages when a parent hardly needs to use any techniques. Five is such an age. The child of Five is for the most part so extremely eager to do the right thing, to please his parents, that "goodness" in many just comes about naturally.

And so, for Five, instead of listing useful techniques as we have for earlier ages, we shall use this chapter to discuss the matter of discipline in general.

Regardless of what we ourselves recommend, it may be of interest to you to know what parents interviewed in a General Mills report actually did use as discipline. Of the several thousand who responded, 52 percent admitted that their chief method of discipline was yelling and scolding. Fifty percent admitted that they spanked. Another 38 percent made the child stay in his room, and 32 percent did

not allow the child to go out to play. Twenty-three percent made the child go to bed. (This doesn't sound too different from the way things were when we ourselves were growing up.)

However, Dr. Fitzhugh Dodson, in the most comprehensive book yet written on the subject of disciplining, *How to Discipline With Love,* considers almost all of these methods undesirable. In fact, he lists as the least effective kinds of discipline: scolding, lecturing, taking away privileges, spanking.

He states specifically, "What punishment power does produce in children and adults is hostility, resentment and the desire for retaliation. *And you simply cannot teach children desirable behavior by arousing these negative feelings.*"

Dodson, like others, believes that children are so desirous of attention that if they cannot get it by doing "good" things, which get them praise and rewards, they will manage to get it by doing "bad" things, and thus getting punished and scolded. To many children, punishment is a better payoff than no attention at all.

So he advises removing the payoff of your attention from all but (1) actions that will actually hurt or endanger the child; (2) actions that will destroy property; (3) actions that plain get on your nerves.

What then can you do when your Five-year-old is behaving in a way that you consider undesirable? Dodson suggests the following:

1. Time out. You send the child to his or her room. This you do not as a punishment, and not in an angry tone, but calmly and in a matter-of-fact way.
2. Environmental control. Even as late as Five, it may be useful to keep your house as child-proof as possible.
3. Allow your child to express negative feelings, but try to help him realize that certain types of behavior just don't get him anywhere.

4. Use a feedback technique. That is, listen to what your child is saying. Formulate in your own mind what it is he is *really* expressing. Feed back to him the feelings he has expressed as you interpret them.

5. Establish a positive reward system. Put your emphasis on the fine things that will happen if your child pleases you and obeys the rules of the house, rather than on what will happen if he is naughty.

6. Even with a Five-year-old you can go a certain way with so-called "contracting." That is, when he behaves in a certain desirable way, or accomplishes tasks he has agreed upon, you in turn will do certain things to please him.

But, if worst comes to worst and your own feelings overcome you and you do end up spanking, don't feel guilty about it. Appreciate that parents have rights, too, and that you, after all, do have the upper hand.

However, best of all in the line of disciplining is knowing a lot about what is and is not reasonable to expect of a Five-year-old. Many things that parents may consider as bad and thus punishable are often simply immaturities. That is, sometimes we expect too much of the child and then punish because he fails to meet our excessive expectations. In a way, this is what this book is all about.

Here are a few special areas in which parents sometimes expect too much. The ordinary Five-year-old does not find it easy to admit wrongdoing. So, if, for instance, you ask him if he was the one who broke the vase (and you are very sure he did), chances are he will say he didn't.

If all evidence suggests that he is the culprit, try asking him *how* he broke it. Often his review of what happened can be very touching: "Well, I was going 'round the corner of the table too fast and I didn't see the vase." Then it may be up to Mother to say, "I shouldn't have left it there; but next time be more careful."

If you feel you *must* punish for the vase breaking (though it would have been best in the first place to have the vase out of reach), do so. But do not, in addition, punish him for lying about whether or not he did it.

Actually, even in less hazardous situations, the ordinary Five-year-old is by no means always truthful. He tries to tell the truth but is not always successful.

Nor can Five always resist taking things that belong to other people. His wants tend to be rather strong and his sense of other people's property is weak. Certainly taking things should not be condoned. But parents should not be surprised if it occurs. The child will need to be quite a bit older before his appreciation of other people's property rights equals his appreciation of his own. (Some Fives show they know they have done wrong by hiding or destroying a stolen object.)

At any rate, prevention is infinitely better than punishment. But if you must punish, do so as calmly as possible. Fortunately, at Five, the child's wish to be good and to do the right things is strong. With luck, much of the time— at least till Five-and-a-half moves on toward Six—there should be pretty much plain sailing.

chapter five
ACCOMPLISHMENTS AND ABILITIES

When your child is an infant, each new accomplishment or ability can be the occasion for excitement and rejoicing. That first word, that first step, that first tooth tend to be greeted as if no such thing had ever happened before.

By the time he is Five, chances are you have become more accustomed to the fact that he has continued to do remarkable things and to add new abilities to his repertoire. You enjoy his enjoyment in these new abilities, but you are a little less anxious if they are late, a little less proud if they are early.

By Five the usual boy or girl has arrived at a good balance between what he would like to do and what he can do. And what he likes most of all to do is *play.* Most Fives play very well indeed. The body is now under a more smooth and skillful control, and therefore most Fives can play without too much adult help or guidance.

Five fits well into the usual kindergarten because he loves the usual kindergarten activities. Cutting, tracing, drawing, pasting, stringing beads, making things with small pieces of paper and cloth—all activities that leave quite a clutter of little snips and pieces—give the Five-

year-old a chance to practice his increasing constructive and creative abilities.

Both girls and boys love blocks—little blocks and big blocks—though they tend to use them in somewhat different ways. Girls build houses for their dolls, whereas boys are more likely to build roads, tracks, bridges, tunnels, trucks, planes, fire engines.

However, both sexes like to build *big* houses with big blocks, or tent houses made of chairs draped with blankets, and then they love to snuggle inside these structures. Often they do not do much once inside, except perhaps talk about how they are now "nice and safe" from whatever they may imagine threatens them on the outside.

Dolls, too, are of great interest to Fives. Naturally they pretend these dolls are babies, and both boys and girls like to play house with their dolls, dressing them, feeding them, putting them to bed or taking them for rides in their carriage. All of this fits into their general love of playing "house," with one or the other of the supposed parents going out to work, the other staying at home to take care of the "housework."

Hospital or doctor play is not as strong as it was at Four, and playing school usually waits till Six.

Both boys and girls enjoy all sorts of gross motor play, with tricycle-riding a general favorite. And Five loves to swing, climb, skip, roller-skate, jump from heights. If climable trees are available, he loves to climb. Jump rope is coming in as well as attempted acrobatics, trapeze tricks, or even walking on stilts. Roller skates and ice skates are favorites with many.

Most play activities are enjoyed by both boys and girls, though girls are likely to prefer sewing, boys, carpentry. Jigsaw puzzles are fun for both, and those children who are spatially well oriented can sometimes master rather complicated patterns.

Others enjoy use of such simple science materials as the magnet, magnifying glass, flashlight, stethoscope. And still others spend a lot of time with games in which they match pictures or forms, or greatly enjoy copying letters and numbers.

Imaginative play, especially playing house, as mentioned, is still very strong, but Five is a factual age and many Five-year-olds like best of all to work with materials, to actually make things, solve puzzles, play games that require a certain application of the intellect. Five is growing up.

READING

Though being read to has for many children been a favorite form of entertainment for several years now, in many it reaches a peak at Five. In fact, there may be nothing your Five-year-old likes better than having you read to him, even though he enjoys spending considerable time looking at books by himself, picking out words he knows, or even in some cases doing a little reading on his own.

Fives still enjoy the humorous, silly, ridiculous books that were such favorites at Four, books like Benton's *Don't Ever Wish for a Seven-Foot Bear* or Kessler's *Do Baby Bears Sit On Chairs?*

They are especially fond of books about animals that act like people, such as Duvoisin's *The Crocodile in the Tree,* or *Petunia's Treasure.* Or they like books that help them develop their increasing intellectual understanding, such as Hafter's *Colors* or his *Yes and No: A Book of Opposites.* They especially enjoy a book like Toni Ungerer's *Crictor,* in which Crictor, a boa constrictor, twists himself into a series of letters and numbers that many Fives enjoy identifying.

Five loves his books, and it is fun to buy books for the child of this age.

MUSIC, RADIO, and TELEVISION

Most Fives seem to prefer their own records to the radio. They like to play their favorites over and over again. Some like to sing or dance as they play. Some Fives already pick

out little tunes on the piano, though this is beyond most. A few like radio, especially if they have their own little portable.

But television is probably, for most, the favorite of these three media. Most if questioned admit that they watch television "a lot," but the amount varies tremendously with the habits of the household. Some parents are still very choosy about the kinds of programs their Five-year-olds watch and the amount of time spent. Others are very lax.

Children themselves say they are allowed to watch as much as they want to, but most parents deny this. Girls claim that they themselves decide which programs to view; boys say that they and their parents decide together. Favorite programs are "Sesame Street," "Mister Rogers," "Bugs Bunny," and the Saturday cartoons. Most dislike the news, soap operas, and "scary" programs.

Girls make the following characteristic remarks about their television viewing: "I'm a TV freak!"; "I can watch anything I want to except mean things"; "I love cartoons"; "My father loves TV, too"; "I only watch it when I come in from play. It would only hurt my eyes if I watched more."

Boys say: "My mother doesn't let me watch so much"; "Sometimes nobody's home when I come home from school so I can watch all I want"; "My father and I watch baseball games together"; "Sometimes they leave me alone and sometimes they tell me to stop."

CREATIVITY: SPONTANEOUS STORIES

Smooth on the surface, but possibly with somewhat stormy depths—this is the child of Five. And especially as he or she moves on toward Five-and-a-half and Six, his earlier smooth surface behavior may be more and more frequently disturbed.

Though certainly no parent of a young child needs to borrow trouble, it is often useful for those dealing with Five-year-olds to realize that the "angelic" behavior so frequently observed may be achieved at a price. Glimpses below the surface can be revealing, though they should not ordinarily be disturbing to the adult.

Children's songs and stories, which many will verbalize freely if given the opportunity, hint at hidden depths and hidden violence. One nice—and so far as we know reasonably normal—Five-year-old told this story:

> Once there was a little girl. She said "Yeah, my tooth came out. I know the fairy will give me something. She told me she'd give me a little crayon box with some crayons in it." That night the little girl went to sleep and the fairy gave her the crayon box. The little girl thought she'd get nothing else, but the fairy said she'd get something else but she couldn't tell her 'cause it was a secret.
>
> Then the little girl woke up and found eighteen presents under her pillow. She said, "I'm going next week to do all the right things and never do the wrong things." Then she got her Indian knife and killed the Indians because she liked to kill Indians so she could eat them. The Indians were good to eat. They had juice inside them. She liked juice.

Asked why she liked to kill Indians, she replied:

> 'Cause they were bad and might kill her mother. They already killed her daddy.

Actually the death of parents seems to be fairly prominent in the fantasies of the child of this age. So this same Five-year-old girl spontaneously sang this song:

> The Indians killed the little girl's mummy and daddy and her brother and sister. Then she was all alone. No, she wasn't all alone. She went to live with her friend and he had eighteen little chairs and tables. And the mummy and daddy got well.

This is just one little girl. How about Five-year-olds in general? Our own check on spontaneous stories of both girls and boys at Five showed that 70 percent of the girls and 65 percent of the boys told stories with violence as the main theme. The chief kinds of violence mentioned were accidents, aggression, harm to people.

Girls, predictably, told stories about girls or mothers; boys told stories about other boys. Boys were more likely than girls to see their mothers in a positive light. Both sexes saw fathers in a positive light.

The majority of our Fives, though they had moved the scenes of their stories outside the home, still laid them in familiar, neighborhood places. But in spite of the close-to-home locale, in 30 percent of stories by girls and 45 percent of stories by boys, fantasy predominated.

CREATIVITY

Of course, storytelling is not the only way the lovely, lively Five-year-old expresses creativity, since creative expression comes in all shapes and sizes. When many of us think about creativity we think of painting, or possibly of music. We sometimes forget that there are many, many different ways of being creative.

The important thing for parents to do is to make available many different kinds of creative opportunities. If your child should be one who creates best with words, allow him to write, or before he can write, just to talk to you or dictate to you, like the child whose story we have just reported.

But also, especially in the early years, it is important, if you are one who values creativity, to make available to your child such standard materials as fingerpaints, brush paints, and clay. Very simple musical instruments are available even for the very young. Puppets encourage creative dramatic play. Almost no equipment is needed to encourage creative dancing.

In fact, one does not need a tremendous amount of equipment to provide a creative experience for one's Five-year-old. Just as at the earlier ages, simply taking a child on a walk can be a creative experience if you discuss, and encourage your child to discuss, the things you both can see.

For the most part, one does not teach a child to be creative, but one does and should provide materials and opportunities that will encourage any potential creativity. You don't really decide for your child what that will be. Each person has his or her own style.

As Lisa Liepmann points out in her excellent book, *Your Child's Sensory World,* some children are talkers, some touchers, some movers, some smellers, some tasters.

Not every child will copy or take advantage of his parents' aesthetic awareness, but it does help any child if in your household you can provide a certain amount of music, art, a reasonable number of books and other reading material. Their availability will not in every instance produce an artist or creator, but it will encourage any latent ability your child may possess.

To encourage those of you parents who may not consider yourselves to be especially creative (that is, you don't paint, sculpt, weave, or play a musical instrument), we would like to emphasize that one can be creative with words as well as with one's hands. Here are a few suggestions from Milton A. Young's extremely helpful book, *Buttons Are To Push: Developing Your Child's Creativity.* They are, we think, good in themselves, and they may also serve to suggest to you other similar ways of being creative, even if your house or apartment is small and even if you don't have too many of the conventional art materials available.

1. Ask your child to find new uses for simple, everyday things like pencils and paper clips. Encourage silly ideas, imaginative uses.
2. Ask your child to figure out reasons that certain things may have happened. For instance, why did his friend cry? Had the children teased him?

3. Show your child a picture. Suggest that he ask as many questions as possible about it.
4. Ask your Five-year-old to think up ways he might help a friend who had a problem—for instance, that nobody liked him.
5. Ask your child to imagine a well-known thing (a door, a window) functioning as something different from its usual use.
6. Ask him or her to figure out a possible solution to a difficult problem, for instance, say a friend lost or forgot his lunch money.
7. Ask your Five-year-old to tell a story or make up a poem, a song, or a dance.
8. Even though he may seem a little young for it, if your child shows any inclination at all to be a collector, help him start a simple collection. (It could be nothing more elaborate than Christmas cards.)
9. Even a Five-year-old is not too young to play games that challenge the imagination and the ability to think. At Five, some even enjoy a game of checkers.
10. List a group of objects and then ask your child to find a common quality (for instance, tree, squirrel, ant, plant, and fish are all alive).
11. Try Twenty Questions. The child may ask twenty questions to try to guess the word you are thinking of.
12. Show your child a picture for a few seconds. Then remove the picture and ask him how many details he can remember.

In short, there are many different ways that even a Five-year-old can express his creativity and can use his imagination. He may do this by making things with his hands. He may do it with music. He may do it simply with words. The important thing is to find a medium that you and your child enjoy and find comfortable. Don't be inhibited by the fact that you may never have considered yourself an especially creative person. Almost any of us can help a Five-year-old to express creativity in one way or another.

MOTOR BEHAVIOR

And now, how about the body that lies behind all this behavior, that is in fact the basis for all behavior?

Unlike his expansive Four-year-old self, Five is now poised and controlled physically. Posturally he is much less extreme and extensory than he was at Four. He is closely knit. His arms are held near his body. His stance is narrow. Eyes and head move almost simultaneously as he directs his attention to something. He is direct in his approach, facing things squarely. He goes directly to a chair and seats himself.

Gross motor activity is well developed at Five. Although the child of this age may walk with feet pronate, he can walk a straight line, descend stairs alternating his feet, and skip alternately.

His alternating mechanism is put to practice in much of his behavior. As mentioned earlier, he loves his tricycle and is adept at riding it. He climbs with sureness and shows a marked interest in stilts and roller skates.

Five's economy of movement is in sharp contrast to Four's expansiveness. The Five-year-old appears more restrained and less active because he maintains one position for longer periods. But though he plays longer in one restricted place, he is a great helper who likes to go upstairs to get something for his mother, or go back and forth from kitchen to dining room to put things on the table.

He is becoming more adept with his hands now and likes to lace his shoes, fasten buttons that he can see, "sew" wool through holes on a card. He likes to place his fingers on the piano keys and strike a chord.

Handedness is often, though not always, well established by Five, and the Five-and-a-half-year-old can identify the hand he uses for writing. He can usually name his eye, eyebrow, palm, elbow, thumb, and little finger. In block building and similar activities he may alternate the use of hands, but the dominant hand is used more frequently.

And now how about that important bodily aspect of behavior—the child's *teeth?* The tooth fairy does not have too much work to do with the ordinary Five-year-old, but by Five-and-a-half to Six a good many children have erupted their lower central incisors and so she may be very busy leaving money under their pillows.

VISION

Five is as focal visually as in other aspects of his behavior. He seldom feels frustration, because he likes the visual answers he gets. He tends to sit with trunk quite upright, his work directly before him. Approach, grasp, and release are direct, precise, and accurate in simple motor performance.

A Five-year-old is visually aware of the totality of space,

though he doesn't take it in all at once. Rather, he moves from one somewhat restricted spot orientation to the next. Because he is apt to get stuck visually on a focal point, he may need specific instructions to complete any given eye–hand activity.

Five likes and demands specificity of orientation. He likes to color within lines, for instance. Ocular fixation is superior to ocular pursuit. Thus the child may be better at looking than at following.

Visually he is interested in the reality of things, much concerned with reality for reality's sake. He may pay attention to something without looking directly at it. He may either look through an object or even look in a different direction and yet still be aware of the thing one is showing him.

chapter six
THE CHILD'S MIND

We offer a separate chapter on the child's mind, or his thinking, or as it is so frequently called nowadays, his "cognitive ability," because the mind is so popular these days with child specialists. They write about it so much, it is almost as if it had just been discovered.

In our own actual work with children we do not do very much about separating the mind from the rest of the child. In fact, body and mind are not two separate parts of the person, they are merely two different aspects of one and the same thing.

Dr. Gesell's statement still holds: "Mind manifests itself." It manifests itself in almost everything the person does. A child's motor behavior, for instance, his ball throwing, can be as much an example of the mind and body at work as can his verbal expressions or his sense of time or space.

However, since many people identify thinking with speaking, we shall separate some of the abilities that are best expressed verbally from those that are expressed primarily by movements of arms, or hands, or eyes, or other parts of the body. In this chapter we will discuss briefly the child's sense of time, his or her sense of space, sense of humor, reading and arithmetic abilities, stories told spontaneously, sex interests, and creative abilities.

THE CHILD'S SENSE OF TIME

The typical time words used by adults are now well within the child's vocabulary and for the most part he uses them correctly. He no longer confuses past and future. He knows when events of his day take place in relation to each other.

Most Fives can name the days of the week and can answer many customary questions about time, such as "What day is today?" "What day comes after Sunday?" "What day does Daddy (or Mummy) stay home all day?" "How old are you?" "How old will you be on your next birthday?"

Most can tell at what hour they go to bed. Nearly all can tell correctly what day it is, but none can tell correctly what hour it is.

Many Fives are much interested in the calendar and the clock. A few copy the numbers on the clock's face and may read them. Five-year-olds like to play with toy clocks even though they are not too good at telling time. Some do know that they are to do something "when the big hand is at the top" or some such.

But Five is a here and now person. He is not comfortable too far from home either in time or space. His chief time is *now*. It is hard for him to imagine himself as not having existed or as dying. Time for him is largely his own personal time. This does not mean that he is selfish. It just means that he is not tremendously aware.

THE CHILD'S SENSE OF SPACE

Five lives in the now, and he also lives in the here. His total world is rather small spacewise, and he likes to be close to home (close to mother), and to think about things rather close to home. He is extremely focal, though admittedly he can branch out into his own neighborhood with increasing comfort.

He can, in his thinking, move out into his own neighbor-

hood but not much farther. This is one of the many reasons, in addition to the fatigue that busing causes, that Five-year-olds do best if they can attend a neighborhood school and not be bused to some distant and, to them, strange place.

Five's space world may be rather small but he tends to be well oriented within it. He can carry out commands in regard to forward, backward, high, low. He can now cross neighborhood streets by himself and can do errands at a nearby store. And he likes to trace journeys on maps and to make simple maps indicating the route he takes to school, or a map of his school room and the things in it.

Though he likes to go on excursions with his mother,

any interest in distant cities or states tends to be limited to those in which someone he knows lives.

READING AND PRINTING

Five years: Though an occasional child, usually a girl, may actually be able to read at this age, most are still in a very rudimentary stage. They may like to identify word signs such as "Stop" and "Go," or "Hot" and "Cold" on faucets. They may do this in the form of a question: "What does D-O-G spell, Mummy?" Fives definitely look on when being read to.

Most recognize their own first name. Some may like using wooden letters to represent names of people they know, or to identify repetitious phrases or words in familiar books.

Five-and-a-half-years: In many there has been quite a marked improvement in reading in the past six months. By this time many are quite familiar with all the letters of the alphabet, and many are well past the simple spelling out of signs and very simple words characteristic of Five years of age.

Many, especially if reading is being stressed in kindergarten, are already at a preprimer stage and can do quite a bit of fairly substantial "reading," especially if print is large and words are short.

The important thing for parents to keep in mind is that reading should not be pushed. If reading is the child's own spontaneous interest, well and good. But if the child does not show spontaneous interest, let him be.

As for the writing (or actually printing) of letters, most can at least print random letters and many can do better than that. The largest number (though not yet half of all children at Five) can print their first name. By Five-and-a-half, more than half can print at least their first name and a substantial number can print both first *and* last names. Or at least they know what letter their last name begins with.

ARITHMETIC

Five years: The child's sense of numbers has taken a big jump between Four and Five. Now many can count by ones, at least a little way. They are aware of using or not using fingers: "I won't count on my fingers." They also can count as many as thirteen objects. Most can name a penny but not other coins.

Some are beginning to enjoy oral figuring and can add within five, though they may or may not use fingers to help out. Some can write a few numbers from dictation, or may like to copy numbers. They may say, "My numbers don't go to twenty, they just go to ten."

Five-and-a-half years: Even more improvement. Now they can count by ones perhaps to twenty, though they may make errors along the way. They can count objects to twenty.

They add correctly within five as earlier, and now many can also subtract within five. Most can write numbers from one to ten or higher but at this age there tend to be many reversals or omissions. The process is still *very* labored.

When asked about numbers they are apt to express uncertainty: "I'm not sure"; "I don't think I know"; "That one's going to be hard"; "I might miss a few." Or, as a Five writes, he says, "I can't make it. It can't be like that because that's a twelve. Something like that. A two and an o. In front or in back?" Or, "Down like that and over like that. Backward, but it doesn't matter." "My hand gets kinda tired. It's kinda awkward."

LANGUAGE AND THOUGHT

The typical Five-year-old likes to talk. In fact, some mothers complain that their child talks constantly—that it is impossible to get away from the sound of his or her voice. Up to a point, conversation is welcomed and even relished, but admittedly some children do talk too much.

In fact this may be one of the kindergartner's problems. It is hard for him to inhibit his constant conversation.

Language is now meaningful to the child for its own sake. He likes new words, big words. He likes to ask, "What does ——— spell?" Most love to be read to and are excited about the idea that soon they themselves will be able to read.

They appreciate the new-found power that being able to spell out signs and simple words gives them. Some can even define simple words.

Five asks innumerable questions, but they are far beyond the Four-year-old's Why, which is as often used as a stall as a search for information. Five wants to know.

According to the much-quoted Piaget, the child is now still in the "preoperational" stage of thinking. He knows that words represent objects and ideas. He learns that actions have both causes and effects—that is, pushing a switch makes a light go on. But he may still explain outside events in terms of his own wishes and needs: "It rained because I wanted it to." He may even believe that objects and natural events have human thoughts and feelings: "It rained because the cloud was angry."

The child may believe that everything active is alive and that man made everything.

That is, Fives still have some difficulty in distinguishing between fantasy and reality. "It happened by magic" is still an acceptable answer to a Five's question (from his point of view).

The Five-year-old is beginning to try to figure things out for himself. He makes his own generalizations, often based on inadequate evidence. Thus if both his grandfathers die before his grandmothers, he may ask, "Do daddies die first?" Or if by chance he has been told that two certain brown dogs were females and two black ones were males, he may conclude that all brown dogs are female and all black ones male.

Belief in Santa Claus is, of course, still very strong. The child believes firmly, writes letters to Santa, and more or less expects to get what he requests. Belief in God, too, is still very strong, though some talk about him less than just earlier. But many do believe that God is responsible for everything—for instance, if the child falls he may think that God pushed him. Many have a very realistic approach to both God and Santa—believe that they are real persons living in houses.

As to death, their concept is becoming more detailed, accurate, and factual. Some even recognize the finality of death, though it is quite customary at this age to think of it as reversible. Children do recognize that when people or animals are dead they are immobile. Interest in death (unless some immediate and much-loved member of the family dies) tends to be matter-of-fact, intellectual, and relatively unemotional.

SEX

Interest in sex and sex play tends to be considerably less at Five than it was just a year earlier. There is less giggling about bathrooms and bellybuttons, less playing the game of Show. Fives not only tend to be rather unsexy but are often quite modest about both their bodies and their bathroom functions. They know about physical differences between the sexes, but there tends to be much less interest in this than earlier.

Interest in babies varies. Some still think the baby is bought in the store or hospital, but perhaps the majority know that babies grow inside the mother's body. Such children may not quite understand, then, why she has to go to the hospital, if the baby is already inside her. "Why do they need a doctor? Why can't Daddy help?"

There is usually more interest in how and where the baby comes out than in how it got in. Many seem to think it comes out through the mother's navel. There seems to be little connection between the size of a pregnant woman and the fact that the woman has a baby inside her.

Many girls are interested in having babies themselves when they grow up, but they seem to take it for granted that this will all come about in its proper time. Some question this: "When am I going to grow up? When am I going to be a mother?" But others seem quite prepared to wait, believing that if they eat their vegetables and want babies they will one day have them.

Some boys as well as girls believe that they, too, can have babies, though one Five expressed the hope that he didn't already have a baby in him.

Those who take more interest in where the baby comes from to start with are usually quite ready to accept the notion that he came from a seed. As one little Five remarked in introducing his baby brother, "This is my little brother. He came from a seed."

Though sex play between Five-year-olds tends to be less frequent than when they were Four or when they will be Six, some Fives are led into sex play by older children.

A few, too, are told about intercourse by older children. They usually report this to their mothers, but if Mother takes this calmly, children often do not seek a more detailed explanation. They mostly seem to want to know whether the other child was telling them the truth or not.

Most children play freely, in everyday play, with either boys or girls, making no special distinction. There is little of the sex discrimination that will come a bit later.

HUMOR

Five is not a wildly humorous age. The typical Five-year-old is almost too nice to be funny. It's fair to say that

while Six may be quite silly and giggly at times, Five by nature tends to be a rather serious little person. When humor does come in, it is usually self-initiated rather than something that involves reciprocal enjoyment.

That is, Five is not tremendously responsive to humor in others, but now and then he does make his own little joke. He is miles from being ready for practical jokes, but now and then a little verbal slapstick does liven up his days.

People are often humorous about things that seem a little dangerous to them. In years past, daring writers made jokes about religion. Similarly, Five may make jokes to the effect that he is not going to do what his parents tell him to.

"Have you eaten your dinner yet?" asks Father, coming home late. "No, and I'm not going to eat it," says Five, delighted with his daring *pretend* rebellion, for of course he actually has already finished his dinner.

Flashes of humor are seen in the child's own spontaneous stories. Rudimentary as they may be, they show that humor has its beginnings very early. Five likes best of all to say something ridiculous: "Once there was a Pontiac. It was crazy. It was going down the road and no one was in it."

"Fooling" people is also funny to him, though he usually takes pains to explain this: "I was fooling you about not knowing where Aunt Millie's house was."

The incongruous as well as the ridiculous tickles his sense of humor: "The man had underpants on. . . . Even the gunman had underpants on but the other man didn't have any clothes on at all."

Silly language, though it occurs much less than it did at Four, seems funny to the Five-year-old, and minor disasters or misfortunes also tickle his fancy: "The animal lost his tail . . . and he told the owl his doorbell was his tail. . . . So then he pulled it and it came off."

chapter seven
SCHOOL

And now comes a whole new world for the child—one of the biggest adventures in any child's life—the beginning of school.

Of course, many boys and girls have had the privilege of attending nursery school. But a good nursery school adapts its demands to the abilities and inabilities of each individual child.

Kindergarten, in all too many communities, is something else again. In spite of vigorous efforts on our part and on the part of many informed educators, more often than not the custom is that Five-year-olds attend kindergarten, Six-year-olds, first grade.

This works out for many, but for many others it does not. Birthday or chronological age is no guarantee of readiness for school. Our position is that the child's behavior age, not his birthday age, should determine the time of school entrance and of subsequent promotion.

We recommend that all children be screened before they start kindergarten, either by the method we recommend[4] or some other sound behavior or developmental tests.

Such tests aim to determine the age level at which the child as a whole is functioning. They indicate whether a given Five-year-old is ready for an advanced kindergarten, and so presumably for first grade the following year.

If not ready for a full kindergarten, he may be ready for a prekindergarten. Or the tests show if he should remain in nursery school or stay at home for one more year.

It is important for parents to appreciate that the child found young, or immature, on a behavior test is not necessarily lacking in intelligence. A child can be bright for his age and at the same time young for his age. A high IQ does not guarantee school readiness. As Hedges[5] points out clearly, both experience and research have shown that so-called early-entrance programs have not worked out. These programs, tried for a time in many parts of the

country, allowed bright but underage children to start school. Their failure emphasized our point of view—that it takes more than a good intelligence for a child to succeed in school. It also requires a certain maturity.

If your school or community does not provide either a full developmental examination or even a simplified screening program, birthday age can at least be a clue to probable readiness. Most girls do best if fully Five before they start kindergarten; most boys do best if fully Five-and-a-half.

Another practical clue to readiness for kindergarten is

if your Five-year-old seems to you as mature as other Fives you know. Other good clues to school readiness are offered by educators Austin and Lafferty[6] in their practical and sensible list of things any parent can check to find out if a child is ready for kindergarten. The full list includes forty-three questions. According to the authors, if you can answer yes to from forty to forty-three, your child is surely ready for school, and if you can say yes to even thirty-five to thirty-nine of them, he is probably ready.

We give you here, with the authors' permission, the nine questions from this list that they consider the most significant. If your boy or girl is really ready to start kindergarten, you should be able to answer yes to most of them.

1. Will your child be five years and six months or older when he or she begins kindergarten?
2. Can he tell you the names of three or four colors that you point out?
3. Can he draw or copy a square?
4. Can he name drawings of a cross, square, circle?
5. Can he repeat a series of four numbers without practice?
6. Can he tell his left hand from his right?
7. Can he draw and color beyond a simple scribble?
8. Can he tell what things are made of, such as cars, chairs, shoes?
9. Can he travel alone in the neighborhood (two blocks) to store, school, playground, or the homes of friends?

In a full developmental placement program, which we recommend, each child is given a behavior or developmental examination before starting kindergarten. On the basis of this he is placed in an advanced or afternoon kindergarten with the expectation that he will go on to first grade the next year; or in a prekindergarten group with the expectation of spending two years in kindergarten before first grade.

A second examination at the end of the school year

would determine the next year's placement, which might be in first grade, in a prefirst or reading readiness class, or in a second year of kindergarten.

There are certain immature children, especially boys, particularly if they are started early, who will need as many as two or three years—prekindergarten, kindergarten, and/or prefirst grade—before being fully ready for first grade.

This may sound as if we are being super-cautious. But our experience has been that if children are fully ready for first grade when starting it—other things being equal—school should be a success. We believe that perhaps as much as 50 percent of school failure could be prevented or cured by proper grade placement on the basis of behavior age.

Two further lists may help those parents who, lacking the benefit of a behavior examination, may not be quite certain as to whether their son or daughter belongs in a morning or afternoon kindergarten. When space and teachers available permit, the more mature Five-year-old who no longer needs an afternoon nap is often placed in afternoon kindergarten. Those less mature, who still need their nap, go in the morning.

The schools of Cheshire, Connecticut,[7] offer the following lists of characteristics of children ready for morning kindergarten only, and those who may be ready for an afternoon kindergarten.

Characteristics of Children
Ready for Morning Kindergarten Group

1. Immature speech patterns persist.
2. Many cannot separate without crying.
3. Mercurial in behavior. Constantly on the run; can't slow down.
4. Likes all activities that involve movement.
5. Needs frequent change of activity—short attention span.

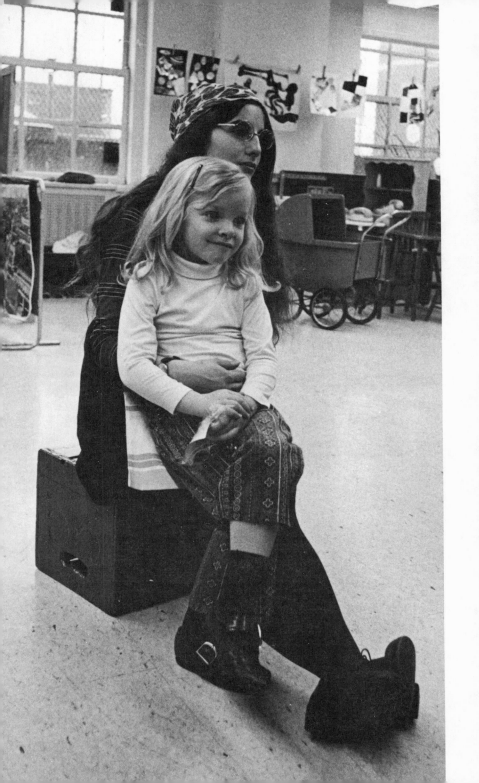

6. Shows limited fine motor ability (i.e., cutting, etc.).
7. Needs more mobile equipment because gross motor activity is preferred.
8. Needs supervision on equipment when he is playing. Forgets safety rules.
9. Lacks desire to conform.
10. Demonstrates aggressive behavior, sometimes disruptive, sometimes destructive. Argumentative.
11. Needs rest but resists settling down.
12. Easily distracted. Often out-of-bounds.
13. Can't accept change in routine.
14. Needs reassurance in anything attempted. Often fails to finish task.
15. Works better in a one-to-one relationship. More time needed for giving directions.
16. Relates best to one or two peers; some isolate themselves.
17. Shows silly, boisterous humor.
18. Poor bladder control evident (especially under stress).
19. Susceptible to contagion—therefore absences more frequent.

Characteristics of Children
Ready for Afternoon Kindergarten Group

1. Still needs the teacher to set him in motion, and may annoyingly ask permission day after day for rather routine activities.
2. An entity unto himself. Separation from mother is easy. "Don't take me"; "I can go by myself."
3. Obedient—able to take in what you say to him and act upon it.
4. Sustains as long as task holds him. Can sustain within the framework of the group.
5. Better organized physically. "He fits"; "His heels are on the floor."

6. Able to cope with table work. Likes to stay within the lines. Likes to copy things.
7. Has given up baby talk substitutions. Now grammatically correct. Asks what words mean.
8. Anticipates next activity and wants to get to it.
9. Gets very involved and very noisy when participating in activities.
10. More consistent in performance; more interested in completion of activity.
11. Better able to participate in group discussion.
12. Able to retain information.

SIGNS OF UNREADINESS

But morning or afternoon may not be the biggest problem. What every parent of a Five-year-old needs to know most is whether his or her child actually belongs in kindergarten at all. Fortunately, those who do not belong have their own good ways of showing it.

The child's teacher will be, or should be, well aware of unreadiness, but here are some suggestions for parents themselves.

One of the plainest ways that children show that they are not ready for kindergarten is by crying and clinging to their mother when it comes time to enter the classroom. Though such behavior is not entirely unheard of even in "ready" children in the first days of school, if it continues for any substantial period of time it should be a warning sign that the child may not be ready for kindergarten.

Certainly any child who has to be dressed and fed and bodily forced onto the school bus is not ready for school.

Unready children find it difficult to take part even in the loose groupings seen in kindergarten. And perhaps most of all, they *bother* the other children. Kindergarten children tend to be permissive about the ways in which their classmates behave. But a child who hurts other children, who throws things, and who destroys the other children's work is saying very clearly that he is not ready, as is the child

who talks too much and constantly interrupts the teacher and the other children.

And then there is a final group who may behave very acceptably in school but for whom the lid blows off the minute they reach home. If school attendance causes home behavior to go to pieces, *something* is wrong.

We maintain that all too many boys and girls are virtually kidnapped into kindergarten long before they are ready, simply because they have reached some arbitrary legal age.

And even if your son or daughter has weathered kindergarten, you cannot be absolutely certain, without a careful behavior examination or a 100 percent guarantee from the teacher, that he or she will then automatically be ready for first grade. It is a big step, and this description reported by the late Catherine MacKenzie in her *New York Times* column gives us a clue as to just how big that step is. This is a Five-year-old boy's description of a visit his class made in the spring to get acquainted with the first-grade room and first-grade children:

"We went in a big room with a stage and the new ones sat in little chairs up front. Then the teachers brought in their kids. Each one had about a hundred. One teacher stood up and looked anxious. Maybe she lost one of hers. I hope I don't get lost.

"The children played Little Black Sambo for us. It was pretty good, but the tigers weren't very fierce. Then they sang. They knew all the words, too. I'd like to learn some of those songs. Then the teacher put on a record and they danced and kicked around on the stage. I hope I don't have to do that.

"We came up then to where the rooms are. They stretch on and on—about a mile—down the hall. You can't see the doors to go out, but somebody said there were doors. They took me up and down the hall twice and then I went by myself to look in the rooms.

"I wonder if they have any books with pictures of your

insides in them. I want to see how vaccination works on your insides so you won't get smallpox. Leonore says you don't get to read for a long time. They make you do coloring and stuff like that for a while.

"She says they talk about trains and airplanes in first grade. I would like to tell the children about the time I was up in an airplane, but I don't think I could talk before so many eyes."

"How do you think you'll like school?" his mother asked him. He replied, "Well, I don't know. I think there's too much. There's a too muchness about it." And maybe there is, at that.

chapter eight
THE FIVE-YEAR-OLD PARTY

The Five-year-old often gives a somewhat deceptive appearance of being exceptionally self-contained and capable. Experience shows, however, that he seems capable because he normally does not try to do too much that is new or difficult. When faced with either the new or the difficult, he may need a surprising amount of assistance. For this reason, the Five-year-old at a party, which presents new situations and opportunities to which he may not be accustomed, may need a good deal of adult help in taking part in games and in carrying out directions. This help should be immediately available, or adults in charge may be surprised to see the usually collected Five go to pieces.

The Five-year-old is not an exceptionally sociable individual. Often if given a free choice he keeps pretty much to himself, especially in a strange situation. He may rely a good deal on a best friend, but just the notion of making friends for its own sake may have lost the charm it held a few months earlier. It is important not to count on too much interaction among guests at a party, particularly until they get warmed up. They may need quite a prolonged warming-up period, so that it will usually work out best to provide initial activity that is more or less solitary and that does not require cooperation. Even once the party is well underway, it is safest not to expect too much collaborative activity.

Getting rid of excessive energy is already something of a problem at parties. (It will be even more so at later ages.) So it is wise to provide at least some games that involve considerable charging about the house.

Fives have a strong property sense but are not as yet capable of keeping track of their property. So now and for the next few years, a good, safe container, clearly marked, needs to be available for their prizes and products. The mother in charge must not only provide this container but should also provide a safe but conspicuous place to keep it. Then each child can keep his eye on his possessions at all times.

Well-behaved as the average Five-year-old is much of the time, a party does not always bring out his best behavior. As at earlier ages, any difficulties or disputes should be smoothed over as easily as possible, without emphasis on what adults may consider "proper" party behavior.

KEYS TO SUCCESS

The key to a successful Five-year-old party seems to be a great deal of planning in advance, even to the extent of overplanning. Have all materials and props ready beforehand. Have games and activities for every minute, and especially for the beginning and end of the party. There is likely to be little interaction among the children and little spontaneous activity. Fives tend to behave in a rather solitary fashion, though there is a little talking and showing each other what they have been given or what they have made.

A big thing seems to be for each to be busy in more or less individual fashion, though all doing the same things. Quite a bit of help or attention is needed from an adult.

Some key theme helps to make the party exciting for the children—for example, a Valentine theme, St. Patrick's theme, an Indian theme.

Number of Guests. Six is probably a good number of guests, because Fives find it hard to wait for turns or attention, as might be necessary when there are more. Preferably have guests of one sex only, though it will work out all right at this age if you have to have both boys and girls. The party described here is a girls' party.

Number of Adults. There should be at least two adults —the mother and one or two helpers.

SCHEDULE

The party can last for two hours. A late-afternoon party ending with refreshments may be best.

4:00–4:15   Guests assemble. This period should be filled with some planned activity, rela-

tively quiet, relatively solitary. Some hand activity is good—making things with pipe cleaners or with clay, for instance. If possible this activity should be set up in advance in a place apart from the main party room or, if necessary, in a corner of the party room.

4:15–4:30   Game of Spider. This gives the children a chance to get acquainted with, or adjusted to, each other without demanding much mingling. Strings are wound around all through the house, in and out of the furniture. Each child follows her own string, winding it onto a little pasteboard spool. Children climb in and out, over and under, but must not move the furniture. Finally, each finds a present at the end of her string. (Presents for this and other games can include any little things, as comb and brush for doll, doll jewelry, play makeup, coin purses, miniature animals, little banks, crayons.)

4:30–5:10   Game of Clues. Clues are written on red paper hearts (if a Valentine party; otherwise on some other item suitable to the kind of party being given). Mother reads aloud the clues, which might be "under something yellow in the living room," "under something green in the front bedroom," etc. Whole group goes charging all over the house to find these successive clues. The last clue leads to a treasure for each person. (This treasure can be material for making something: i.e., Valentine hats and aprons, or calendars, or pot holders, or candlestick holders. Preferably it should be something in keeping with the theme of the party.) All this charging around after the clues, especially if the party is held in a fairly large house, tires children out enough so that they will probably be contented to sit fairly quietly making whatever their material suggests.

5:10–5:15   Marching and record playing. Fives love marching. A birthday march all around the area used for the party can be great fun. A phonograph record, a piano, or the singing of a rousing song can provide the musical background for the march. Simple rhythm instruments for each of the children add to the fun. This is an activity most children like, and gives a further opportunity for working off energy. Or some suitable record, preferably an "activity" record, can be played so that the whole group can join in.

5:15–5:45   Refreshments. The table should be set ahead of time in the dining room with a tablecloth, napkins, and paper plates. Provide simple favors—perhaps a special placecard holder for each child. Children's food tastes at this age tend to be conservative, so don't try anything fancy, or give a choice of foods. A good menu includes small sandwiches, milk, and some crunchy food like carrot sticks or celery. End with cake and ice cream.

5:45–6:00   Some planned activity for after food—something to do till all parents arrive. Coloring or some other sedentary activity is good.

HINTS AND WARNINGS

It is very important to have all the many materials ready in advance, so that there will be no long waits. Fives need to be entertained steadily; they are not good at improvising, at least not while at a party.

It is also important to plan something that will get them started and keep them occupied till all the children arrive, without much demand on them for spontaneity or sociability.

Be careful not to let expenses get out of hand. Remember that for each favor or gift you must multiply by the number of guests. Also remember that children of this age like to make things but need a good deal of help.

Be *sure* to provide a marked bag or container for their presents and favors. They become very much upset if they think their "things" are getting lost or mixed up with other people's.

Remember that the Five-year-old party is very important to Fives, perhaps even more than the Four-year-old

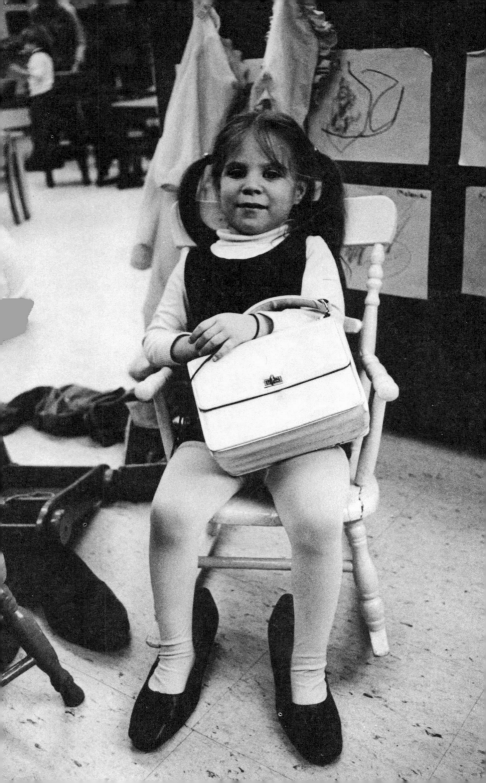

party is to Fours. The child may have anticipated it so long that he or she may be overexcited, and then you may have to overlook some less than ideal behavior on the part of the host or hostess (or of some of the guests).

If the party is given for boys instead of girls, remember that boys tend to move around more and need a good chance to be physically active and boisterous. Thus parties for boys need to go faster. They need to move from one activity to another more rapidly than girls do. And remember that boys do not as a rule have as good party manners as girls do.

chapter nine
INDIVIDUALITY

And now we'd like to give you our most important warning. Always keep in mind that every child is an individual, different in many ways from every other child living— even from his or her own identical twin.

So as we've said before, when we tell you that Five is calm and serene and Six is something else again, this doesn't mean that *all* children at these ages will behave exactly in the ways we have described in our books.

The stages we tell you about, we believe in. We truly believe that the characteristics (or as some, less friendly, have described them, the caricatures) of ages as we describe them are *on the average* true. But that definitely does not mean that all children at any one age are alike.

TIMING

To begin with, there is the matter of timing. Perfectly normal boys and girls can be as much as six months or a year ahead of or behind the schedule we describe. So for some, the wildness of Four does not calm down at the usual Five. It may be well on toward Five-and-a-half before some children calm down. Or the "goodness" of Five may be uninterrupted in some until well on into the child's sixth year.

Conversely, some, again quite normal, may be six months or a year ahead of the kinds of behavior we describe.

This, if you look at the age change chart on page 7, will be seen as a sort of *vertical* displacement—the child is ahead or of behind the behavior we describe as typical of birthday age.

But there is another extremely important variation that is less often considered, and that is *horizontal.* Some children hit the stages at just about the ages we have described. But, depending on their own basic personality characteristics, their midline may be displaced either way to the right (as you look at the chart) or way to the left.

EQUILIBRIUM VS. DISEQUILIBRIUM

Those lucky children whose midline may be thought of as way to the right are by nature at all times basically in good equilibrium. Even when their behavior breaks up slightly, when things are not going quite as comfortably as they might be, they still make out rather well. Even at ages of what is for them disequilibrium, things aren't really too bad.

At the opposite extreme are those whose midline is way to the left. Such children may seem to be almost always in some disequilibrium. Even at their best and smoothest ages, things may not go too well for them.

As one mother put it, "You said that when he was Three he would be easier to live with. Well, he was a tiny bit easier, for about two weeks, and then right back to being the same old Harry." Exactly. Even at his best, such a child does not attain any marked degree of equilibrium. We don't say he is a born loser. We just say that, for some, life at all ages tends to offer considerable difficulty.

DIFFICULT CHILDREN VS. EASY ONES

Dr. Stella Chess, who has contributed a good deal on the general topic of individuality, confirms our own feeling that there are difficult children and easy ones.[8] As she points out, a personality pattern that holds a serious risk of behavior problems combines irregularity in biological functions, predominantly negative (withdrawal) responses to new stimuli, nonadaptability or slow adaptability to change, frequent negative mood, and predominantly intense reactions. Such children are slow to warm up.

Even as infants they are difficult. They are slow to give up their night feedings; find it difficult to fall into a predictable schedule of behavior. And even at the usually benign age of Five, they are not particularly easy to live with. So the glorious age of Five that we describe in this volume may not seem quite as glorious to you if you have a boy or girl who was born, so to speak, on the dark side of the moon.

In contrast, many of you are fortunate enough to have what may truthfully be described as easy children. At all ages they seem comfortable with themselves and with others. They respond quickly and easily and even eagerly to change. They show a predominantly positive mood. They are good in strange places; they are good with strange people. They easily accept new foods or new clothing. They love life.

In such a child, Five may express itself in all its glory.

WITHDRAWAL VS. EXPANSION

And now let's offer a second chart, similar in appearance to the one on page 10, but marked to show a different kind of alternation. This one attempts to illustrate the way behavior changes, as the child grows older, from a characteristic outgoingness and readiness to meet new situations with enthusiasm to a characteristic withdrawal and tendency to stay close to home and to avoid new situations.

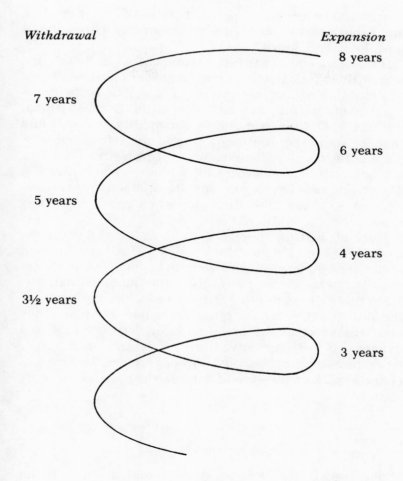

Figure 2

Alternation of Ages of Withdrawal and Expansion

In general we expect expansion around Three, Four, Six, and Eight years of age; withdrawal around Three-and-a-half, Five, and Seven.

Here again comes the fact of each child's individuality, which alters though it does not negate our chart. In almost any child we expect that certain ages will be more outgoing than others. But, once again, if you adjust the mythical midline to fit your own child's personality, you will find that for some the midline is way to the left of average. Such children, like the ones whom Chess first describes, are basically characterized by a tendency to withdraw. They avoid new people and new situations whenever possible; meet them with difficulty when meet them they must.

Much of the time they tend to concentrate on the negative side of life. "My lousy luck," they will tell you. And sad to say, their luck often does seem to be lousy, even at ages usually characterized by equilibrium and outgoingness.

For those whose midline is displaced to the right, toward the side of outgoingness, quite the opposite is true. They meet the world with dash and vigor, love the new and dangerous, welcome adventure. They live in a larger world because they welcome new experience. And even at characteristic ages of withdrawal they withdraw only slightly.

CONSISTENT VS. INCONSISTENT BEHAVIOR

One special aspect of personality that we have found useful for parents to think about is the consistency or inconsistency of a child's behavior.

The extremely stable child tends to behave consistently. One can more or less, within reason, know what to expect of him. Though any child's moods vary, some children are rather predictably sunny, others gloomy. Some are *always* ready for anything new; others *always* cling to the tried and true. And so for whatever characteristic one may have in mind, some children *always* behave like themselves; others are unpredictable.

In the early years we sometimes think of four major fields of behavior: motor, adaptive, language, and personal-social. The more consistent children tend to perform more or less evenly in all four fields. That is, they are above age, at age, or below age expectations in all four fields.

Others are uneven. They have high points and low. As they grow older, for instance, they may be very good in reading and other associated language behaviors but very poor in anything that requires motor skills. Or vice versa.

Clearly, the child whose behavior is consistent has a tremendous advantage over the one whose behavior is variable and unpredictable. Life is easier not only for the child, but for those around him (parents and teachers) if he can count on himself and others can count on him for more or less a certain kind of performance. Inconsistency tends to make difficulty for all concerned.

TWINS

And now one final consideration. We mentioned at the start of this chapter that every child living is different in many ways from every other child, even his or her own identical twin.

Much of the early work Gesell did centered on twins. It was our observation that even the most highly identical twins each had his or her own strong individuality. One typical pair of girl twins, Alice and Rachel, were so much alike that as young as seventeen weeks of age, in the course of a severe illness, they not only exhibited the same physical symptoms but experienced identical temperature rises at the height of their illness.

Height and weight increased over the years at an almost identical rate. On intelligence tests their scores remained always within five IQ points of each other for the first twenty years of life. On one occasion on a spelling test at school they not only missed the same words but misspelled them in the same way.

In general, behavior timing and nature of responses were almost identical. And yet, for all this similarity, there were real differences between these girls that appeared early and continued late. The right-handed twin, Alice, was the quicker of the two whenever there *was* a difference in timing. If an object was to be approached, whether by hand or by the whole body, Alice approached it more directly. Her twin, Rachel, reached for things with a curving approach and moved less directly toward any object. At all ages Alice was more interested in objects than in people; Rachel was just the opposite.

Most conspicuous was their manner of drawing. Quick, clear, and direct, Alice would draw a person with a straight mouth and straight hair. Rachel tended to draw a smiling mouth and curly hair. Alice drew a house with straight smoke coming out the chimney; Rachel's smoke was curly.

These differences persisted. In seventh grade, Alice won in competitive racing but Rachel was the one who had a boy friend. After high school they both got a job at the same dress shop. Alice did alterations in the back of the shop; Rachel preferred a salesgirl job in the front.

All these things and more must be kept in mind by any reader of this book. We can tell you a good deal about what the average or more or less typical Five-year-old is like. But there will be many things about your own Five-year-old that will make him different from any other child of his age. *Every child is an individual!*

chapter ten
STORIES FROM REAL LIFE

HOW TO GET RANDY TO EAT

Dear Doctors:

We have a Five-year-old son, Randy, and it seems to both his father and me that he has hardly eaten a bite since he was weaned from the breast to solid food. I realize that he must now and then eat something or he wouldn't be alive; but it isn't much.

Do you have any general advice for the parents of a noneater?

We're glad you asked. So much attention nowadays is being put on the right diet and on getting children to eat foods that will not actually harm them that the specialist seems almost to have forgotten that for some children it isn't a question of what they eat so much as will they eat.

Good up-to-date advice is given by Dr. Paul S. Graubard in his new *Positive Parenthood* (Bobbs-Merrill 1977). He points out that many feeding problems start at a very early age. Somewhere after one year of age the (often) hearty infant appetite declines. Parents don't like this and often (mistakenly) urge their children to eat more.

And thus the seeds for a nice little problem are laid. Also, young children sometimes balk at eating because of irritability or illness or even because too much attention is paid to a brother or sister. Dr. Graubard suggests some specific steps that you can try, as follows:

Communicate to Randy, nonverbally if necessary, that you expect him to eat and will provide him with all the good food he wants. At the same time, make it clear that the choice of eating or not eating is entirely his, and that you will not make him eat or even pay attention to him if he does not eat.

Don't let him snack, and serve food only at mealtimes. Give very small portions and, within reason, serve foods that he currently likes best. Don't worry (at first) about a balanced diet.

Note carefully when he eats most. Keep records if need be. Your records may show that he eats best when you're not there in the room.

When he eats a little, give a tiny bit more, but just a tiny bit. If he wants to dawdle and play with his meal let him, but at the end of thirty minutes take his plate away and let him know that the meal is over and there will be no food till next meal.

Most reluctant eaters get upset when they see that their parents are no longer making a fuss about their not eating.

But what if Randy doesn't eat foods that you consider essential to his health and well-being? Then follow Grandma's law. In this case, "You may have your ice cream if you finish your spinach." It doesn't need to be ice cream, but even for a poor eater there is usually something that he likes. Make his having that something contingent on his eating just a tiny bit of something else that you think he needs.

A NEGLECTED FIVE-YEAR-OLD REVOLTS AGAINST PARENTS

Dear Doctors:

I have a real problem with my Five-year-old son, Ike. He is terrible to his year-old baby sister. He makes a dreadful fuss when I tend to her and stamps and hollers while she is trying to sleep. If she pulls out the TV plug while he is watching TV he slaps and pinches her or knocks her down so that she falls and bumps her head.

We got him a dog, since we live in the country where there really aren't any children for him to play with. But he seems to enjoy punishing his dog more than playing with him.

He adores his father. But my husband is mostly tired and grouchy. Not only is he not interested in playing with Ike, but he doesn't seem to know how. What can I do to make my son treat his sister and his dog better and to be a happier little boy?

Your son seems to be telling you, rather clearly, that he is not mature or responsible enough to be left alone with the baby. He clearly is an unhappy little boy who feels that the baby's coming has changed his life considerably for the worse. That he even mistreats his dog shows the depth of his feelings that he has been pushed aside. He is miserable and he's going to make even the dog miserable.

He apparently does not have too much ability to entertain himself, few friends are available, you are busy, and his father either isn't there or doesn't know how to play with him. That really doesn't add up to a very busy, happy, satisfactory life, does it?

Is there any possible way that you could get a baby-sitter for the baby a few times a week, and then spend your free time doing interesting things with your son? Take him on walks or excursions, read to him, play with him. Have the day or half day when the sitter is there be "Ike's Day" and let him choose (within reason) what you will do.

There are many fathers like your husband. They are either not at home, too busy or too tired to play with a preschooler, or they just don't know how. To people to whom playing with children comes naturally, this may seem odd. But many men feel big and foolish and unhandy when around very small children.

It looks as though you are going to have to suggest and

set up very simple activities that they can carry out together. No miracle is going to solve your boy's problems. But if you could spend a little more time with him alone, take him to visit friends when you can, try to help his father play with him a little better, and protect the baby from him a little more, his own life will not be so empty. Then he will have a few more of the satisfactions that he so desperately needs.

HANDLING FIVE-YEAR-OLD GIRL WHO RESENTS
YOUNGER SISTER REQUIRES GREAT PATIENCE

Dear Doctors:

Our older girl, barely Five, is causing me considerable concern and worry. Having located her thumb when she was five days old, it seems as if it's scarcely left her mouth since. She is a high-strung and sensitive little girl. Before our younger daughter was born two years ago, Nancy firmly insisted that she didn't want a baby brother or sister, just "a Baby Door"! (The doctor said she apparently didn't fear competition from a door!)

Having no chance for many playmates, the Two-year-old and Five-year-old are together a great deal. Once in a while they get along nicely, but since the Two-year-old is very aggressive and leads off with slaps or her teeth, we have some wild times.

But our Five-year-old usually says, "I wish we'd never had her," or "Who can we find to kill her?" She seldom strikes back, but after a battle goes into another room, and how she sucks her thumb and strokes her hair!

Also recently she has started to calmly fix a bottle for herself, eats messy foods with her fingers, and in general she seems to be retrogressing to her sister's level. Apparently it's just fun, but I notice she quickly hides a bottle if anyone comes to the door.

What can we do about such jealousy that lasts so long? How can we handle it?

This jealousy of her sister undoubtedly made your daughter worse, but in general we would say that her behavior is not caused primarily by jealousy. This kind of behavior happens very often in high-strung, highly intelligent children who have difficulty organizing their emotions.

Since she is now Five years old, you may be already coming into that more difficult period of Five-and-a-half to Six, when the child regresses to babyhood even if there isn't another child in the family. The presence of the younger child makes her regress more fully, but this behavior is quite common in only children, too.

We would recommend letting her go back to babyhood. Satisfy this strong tendency toward regression. Let her know that it is perfectly all right, within the family, to do this. Plan with her about it, if you like.

Often if it is planned out and allowed (that she will drink from a bottle, etc.), it is much less interesting to the child than if she thinks it is not permitted. Then she may become more interested to go ahead and try to behave more maturely.

Try having a bedtime chatting period with her, either you or her father. Talk over the day. If you like, discuss that it is all right to feel like a baby and to be a baby. Tell about yourself as a young child or a baby. Even tell her of your own badness—this sometimes makes the child herself feel less alone and less bad.

All of this will not cure her, but it may make things easier for her. Later, school will absorb a great deal of this energy and take her mind off her sister.

FIVE-YEAR-OLD SHY BOY CAUSES PARENT CONCERN—
HE NEEDS SPECIAL HANDLING

Dear Doctors:

My son, Don, is five years old, and actually I'm not sure if I have a problem or not, but I am kind of worried about it. I would like to know if my worries are necessary or if I'm making a mountain out of a molehill.

Don is very shy and has always been. I'm told that his daddy was very shy as a boy. Today kind of brought things to a head. Don went to a birthday party. Of the eight children present, Don knew only two. He seemed utterly miserable and didn't want to eat. He didn't want me to leave the room and if I did he followed. When he followed me into another room I scolded him for being a baby, and I could bite my tongue out for doing it.

Don't get me wrong. I don't want to change him, I just want to know how to handle or not handle his shyness. When he and the little girl next door play together he is OK, though he doesn't like to eat there. . . . He is taking an interest in letters and numbers, but if what he wants to learn is a little harder and takes a little more concentration than he had figured on, he says, "Let's learn some other day." He doesn't like Sunday School and I'm pretty sure it is because I can't stay with him. What should I do?

From all you say it does not seem that you face a real problem with Don's shyness. Of course, any degree of shyness presents a problem of a sort, but this one seems to us to be well within normal limits. With boys like this, we usually advise starting where the child is. That is, we do not sit around thinking how nice it would be if he were bolder, or friendlier, or better at greeting people and associating with others. We merely accept him for what he is and then try very slowly and gently to pull him a little bit out of his shell.

Set up very simple, easy play situations, perhaps with one other young child, and with you in the immediate offing. As to adults, don't expect him to do much in the way of returning their greetings for at least another two years. His lack of response is undoubtedly due to a combination of a rather diffident shyness, some immaturity, and the fact that it is difficult for many children of this age to speak up when greeted by adults. You comment that his daddy was shy as a young child. Don probably comes by this quite naturally.

Don't begin to judge a child by the way he acts at a birthday party. Many children behave badly at parties.

There are many boys, like your son, who don't like to eat away from home, and there seems to be no real reason why he should be forced to. You do not say whether he is in school this year. He is the kind of boy who would profit greatly by a good Four-year-old nursery-school experience. He doesn't, at this time, seem ready for kindergarten. He sounds like one of those quite bright boys who will do far better if he enters first grade when he is fully six, and perhaps more, before he starts.

PARENTS MUST BE PATIENT WHEN HANDLING
ACTIVE MESOMORPHIC SON

Dear Doctors:

After reading about the mesomorphic child, I have been so much better able to cope with our son. Not only does one have to cope with the child, but with well-meaning friends and relatives who maintain that there isn't such a thing as "types" of children and all a child needs are severe spankings to straighten him out.

We adopted our son, Butch, when he was ten days old. He is Five now, robust of build and of unlimited energy. He has always been very loud in talking and noisy when walking or playing; positively cannot sit or stand still; is aggressive; insists upon destroying everything in sight. His interest span is very short. He seems impervious to pain to himself or others; is very rough with animals; slow to toilet train; constantly getting into trouble; will try your patience to the nth degree and seems to be always asking for disciplinary measures by his actions. He is extremely affectionate. He must play with older boys as he is too rough for those his own age.

Butch was examined by a psychiatrist when Two-and-a-half years of age, who advised strong disciplinary measures until he is approximately Eight, when he would settle down. He also stated that Butch is a near-genius, but we have not noticed this. We are concerned about him entering first grade next fall due to the fact that he can't sit still and his interest span is so short. Also he requires such firm discipline.

We must compliment you on your objective understanding of your son. And on your successful coping with what is actually a difficult kind of personality. We often say that with children like Butch you need an assembly line of at least five people to take care of him. As one fatigues, another one takes over.

We would suggest that you give him as much as you can of the music and dancing you tell us he likes. Set aside an hour after supper when he can really be creative in the dancing realm.

As for school next year, he is on the too-young side for first grade but will probably need some of the intellectual stimulation that first grade would give him. Often these boys calm down as soon as they come into the more specific learning situation. Could you arrange now for a reduced kindergarten attendance? One and a half to two hours is often long enough for these boys to be in school and also long enough for their teacher to put up with them.

Would the school allow you to take him out on Wednesdays, when you could have a planned program at home? Do something alone with him during his time off. Then plan time when you give him workbooks preparatory to reading, play with numbers, learning his letters, etc.

It is not easy to rear a boy like this. He may give the impression of a much higher intelligence than his achievement will show. But eventually as he moves into his own choice of interests, his achievement will quite likely be more definite and satisfactory.

MOTHER EMBARRASSED BY MANNERS SON EXHIBITS
IN PRESENCE OF GUESTS

Dear Doctors:

Could you write some articles for the newspaper on the subject of "how to teach children to talk nicely and intelligently with older people."

My son always embarrasses me when older people try to talk to him. He wriggles around, his hands start sweating sometimes, and he ends up by saying, "I don't know, you knucklehead!" Or he says nothing at all.

He talks our ears off at home, and he is a good boy. He is Five years old and was always shy when younger. Now he is more talkative, but it is at the wrong time. He always interrupts when his elders are talking to each other.

Are there some books you can refer me to?

We don't know of any books on the subject you mention. Actually, we did have to laugh at your description of your son with company. It is so typical of children his age and actually may get worse when he is Six. After that, it should improve.

The main thing right now is to protect him from company—the kind that doesn't understand children—and vice versa. And to expect very little. Sometimes when company comes, if one person could go with him to his room where his toys and books are, you might find that he will do very well alone with that one person. But most Five-year-olds, at least in this culture, are not very good about being quiet, looking right at the person, talking sensibly. It takes a lot of time before most children come up to their parents' expectations in these respects.

FIVE-YEAR-OLDS FOLLOW "THE RULES,"
WHICH THEY ACCEPT WITHOUT QUESTION

"That's a very bad man!"

Grandmother and Five-year-old Debby were in the railroad station waiting for their train. Grandmother turned to look at the not particularly vicious-looking man whom Debby was pointing out.

"What did he do?" she asked her granddaughter.

"He's a litterbug!" whispered Debby.

This simple incident emphasizes the vulnerability of the average preschooler to the teachings and examples of her mentors, so far as moral precepts are concerned.

The young child may (or may not!) be "polymorphous perverse" (or just generally wicked), as Freud would have it. And certainly a child does have to develop to a certain stage of maturity before he can maintain complete truthfulness and thoughtfulness of others.

But most of us who have tried know with what relative ease we can put across such simple concepts as that it is bad to be a litterbug, a fussbudget, or a tattletale. In fact, Munro Leaf may have done quite as much as all the Sunday School classes in presenting simple, clear, amusing stereotypes of the good and bad way to do things.

We frequently emphasize that so far as most important ethical concepts are concerned, it is necessary to wait for just plain development. For instance, the ordinary Six-year-old finds it difficult to admit wrongdoing. Even as late as nine years of age many perfectly nice children still blame others for their own wrongdoing, especially if they think they can get away with it.

However, that doesn't mean that we have to wait, or should wait, until the child is fully ready and able to take advantage of our teaching. You can start at any time—the important thing is just not to expect too much response too soon. But to make these teachings most effective, many parents find that very simple precepts, and consistent example, are far more effective than long moralistic discussions of what people "ought" to do.

"It's the rule," a Five-year-old told us cozily. "If we leave the table before we're through, we can't come back." And she stayed at the table!

SPECIAL HELP MAY BE NEEDED FOR GIRL
WHO REBELS AT LEARNING TO WRITE

Dear Doctors:

Before my daughter started kindergarten, like many mothers I tried to teach her to write letters and numbers. At first she was cooperative, but shortly before school started she would have no part of learning. I thought the teacher might have a better effect on her. And as school progressed, she brought home workbook papers that were practically perfect. But near the end of the year I learned to my dismay that she still would not learn to write her name for the teacher.

This fall she will be in the first grade. I've been trying to help her learn to write the alphabet which they must know for reading, and I'm having the same results. She refuses to learn or write after just a few minutes of working. If this same attitude is going to exist next fall in first grade, it is going to make things awfully hard for her.

Are there other children like this? What happens to them? I want to help her at home somehow to make the going a little easier when she gets to school. My family, my husband's, and all our children have been excellent students, and my daughter's behavior makes me ashamed. Where have I failed?

We do have two suggestions.

First: Every mother learns, sooner or later, not to compare one child to others in the family. Each child must and will progress at his own pace. The classroom honors that have come to others in the family are no guarantee that your daughter will ever make the honor roll. School yourself not to be ashamed if she turns out not to be an outstanding—or even a good—student.

Second: Your letter indicates that your daughter may not be ready for the first grade next fall. Her resistance may be purely temperamental, but often this kind of resistance shows up in a child who seems ready for a given educational task but isn't. If she's to succeed in school, a child can't just be able (in parents' and teachers' estimation); she must be willing, too.

Sometimes refusals to do schoolwork are unnecessary, and can be overcome. But often they're the child's way of telling you that the demands of the situation are too great for him. We'd be interested to know if your daughter shows any spontaneous interest in letters and learning. Is she interested in road signs? If she doesn't pick up "Stop" signs, we'd question her readiness for the first grade.

Advance help in the summer, before school, can some-. times help a child sharpen up abilities that she actually has. But it can't put abilities into her.

At least discuss with her teacher the possibility of her not being ready for the first grade. We strongly suggest a good talk with both teacher and principal to see what they think about the situation.

YOUNGSTER FRIGHTENED BY WITCH HE SAW
IN *SLEEPING BEAUTY*

Dear Doctors:

We have what we consider a great problem. About two months ago our son, Joey, who is almost Five-and-a-half years old, saw *Sleeping Beauty*. Since then he wakes up crying each night and comes into our bed. Previously he was a wonderful sleeper.

We have sat on his bed and have tried to reassure him that a witch is not real. We have tried not permitting him to enter our bedroom. All this to no avail. In order to get a little sleep we now take turns sleeping with him. He is a restless sleeper.

Another event took place recently. We had another baby who sleeps in our room. I claim this is the real reason Joey wants to be with one of us, not the witch that started his wakefulness. My husband disagrees, as his fears and waking started the night he saw the picture.

During the day he is fine. He goes to kindergarten and helps with the baby. We are moving to another state soon. The baby will have a room and Joey his. I wonder if this will help, though I suppose that a new neighborhood and new school might create other problems. Please advise us, as all three of us need sleep badly.

It is, of course, quite possible that the coming of the new baby, your son's age of Five-and-a-half, and perhaps his rather sensitive temperament have all contributed to your present problem. But in our opinion, your husband is probably correct. We suspect that it may well have been the witch in *Sleeping Beauty* that started him off, and that without it he might have managed to survive the other factors.

We have found that there is a definite danger in some of these scary TV broadcasts for quite a few children below eight years of age. We have had many reports of difficulties such as yours caused by these programs. People think that because they are fairy stories, they are fine for children. Actually, many of them are not. Children respond much more strongly to them than many parents realize.

There is quite a difference between witches and such in books and witches seen on TV. In general, we do not find fairy stories harmful to the average child, but parents should make a careful evaluation of their children's stamina, and the probable violence of the program, before allowing them to watch.

As to your own specific problem, time, of course, is on your side. Joey will almost certainly outgrow this kind of fear eventually. Moving to the new house may set up a whole new kind of response to nighttime and sleeping. You may find that you have to "exorcise" the possible witches, and that this use of magic may help to reassure your son.

However, it is important to acknowledge the reasonableness of his fear and to give him the support he seems to need. As you say, a new home, neighborhood, and school may create other problems, but they may express themselves in other ways, and you may at least get a little more sleep.

BAD-BEHAVING CHILD NEEDS
A LOT OF HELP TO CHANGE

Dear Doctors:

My Five-and-a-half-year-old son Terry is a regular Jekyll-and-Hyde personality. He has many good, lovable characteristics, but he can be an absolute monster. The neighbors can't stand him—he strikes out at other children in the most vicious manner or, for instance, grinds dirt into other children's faces. On the rare occasions when I have to take him to the store he lies on the floor and kicks and screams if he can't have everything in sight. Do you think he is emotionally disturbed, and can you advise me? My doctor feels he'll outgrow this.

We have indeed known boys like Terry, and we agree with your pediatrician that time changes many things and that such boys often do finally turn out all right. But time alone doesn't do it. You have to help.

Gradually, we hope, Terry will learn to control his own violent temper, but for the next few years you're going to have to help him. If possible, keep him out of supermarkets and other complicated public places, at all costs. This may be hard but—you wouldn't feed him food that really poisoned him. And to him, right now, a supermarket is a poisonous situation.

He must somehow learn (gradually) that certain behavior will not be tolerated. If he can't play without hurting people then he will have to stay inside with you. A boy like this has to learn that he must earn the right to play with others, go to school, etc. (So far as school goes, you may have to tell him every morning what he will and won't do.)

Rules, for a boy like this, must be strict, clear, and pretty much inflexible. These boys function best in a simple situation where they know the rules.

Children like Terry often respond well to a male baby-sitter. A high school boy would be very good if you could find one. We imagine that Terry gets along well with older boys and girls, and with adults. This is usually true of boys like this. Older people like their sturdy, manly ways, and they, in turn, don't try out their worst behavior with older people. (Except, of course, with their mothers.)

When Terry is a little older, you may find that summer camp will be very successful. These active, aggressive boys tend to be competitive, and they like to succeed and to win out over others. Camp can provide such a situation.

Terry won't change overnight. But he will improve if you can manage to keep his surroundings clear and simple, and if you can help him to understand what the rules are. Boys like this just don't seem to have good sense about what kind of behavior is and is not permissible. You have to spell things out for them.

Above all, don't lose hope.

IS IT ADVISABLE FOR A FIVE-YEAR-OLD
TO HELP CARE FOR NEW BABY?

Doctors worked without rest trying to save the life of Robin Dean, Five, who was badly burned while helping her mother heat milk for a baby brother. Mrs. Dean said Robin's clothes caught fire as she was heating milk for a younger brother. The mother said she was talking on the phone in another room when she heard the girl's cries and found her rolling on the floor in flames.

The Five-year-old tends to be, by nature, extremely co-operative. He likes to help Mother, and particularly likes to help with the baby. It is quite natural for a busy mother to accept any and all offers of help.

Also, Five-year-olds, being less adventurous than they will be even in another year, much of the time do not attempt things that will be too difficult for them. Thus they give an impression of being far more capable than they actually are.

So you can hardly blame a busy mother for allowing a cooperative and seemingly capable Five-year-old to help a little around the house. Fine—there are situations where it does seem safe. A little sweeping, a little bedmaking seem like fairly hazard-free domestic situations.

But cooking—no. Holding the baby—no (unless safely seated in a big overstuffed chair or sofa and mother close by). The Five-year-old's offer to help, kindly as it may be intended, must not always be taken at face value. He and the baby must both be protected. It was obviously a serious mistake to talk on the phone in another room while a Five-year-old heated milk for the baby.

SOME YOUNG CHILDREN ARE NOT ACCEPTED BY GROUPS UNTIL THEY'RE OLDER

Dear Doctors:

I feel terrible to admit this, but nobody seems to like my boy, Dixie. He just isn't accepted by his playmates. He is now Five-and-a-half. In the morning the pre-schoolers ignore him and refuse to let him into their yards. They won't even give him a chance.

And in the afternoon, when he comes home from kindergarten, the Six- and Seven-year-olds don't want him; and if he does manage to join them, they end up beating him up.

His teacher says he gets along fine in school and even on the playground. Also, he gets along with his younger brother. And if just one child comes into our house he can play with him all right. It's just outside that he isn't accepted.

What can I do to help him? It's really getting me down to think that nobody will play with my child. Should I protect him, or force him to go out and make his own way?

Of course, you feel terrible. We all want our children to be popular. Unfortunately, popularity is in some cases a rather mysterious thing. Sometimes it's hard to figure why some children are always surrounded by friends, others always relatively isolated.

Fortunately, Dixie does get along with the children at school. This is not only encouraging, but it gives you a clue that so far he seems to need a rather formalized social situation. So long as there is an adult more or less in charge, he seems to make out pretty well.

So far, we must admit, he seems unready to handle free, unsupervised play. Even very young children, as in your neighborhood, seem to recognize the child who isn't sure of himself. And instead of being kind and helping him, they very often, as in Dixie's case, reject him.

It seems that for the present he may have to content himself with selected kinds of social situations: school (in and out), home with his brother, and home with one selected child. Gradually, we're certain he will broaden out. But even when he does he may always be a boy who does best with one close friend at a time rather than as a member of a large group.

FIVE-YEAR-OLD BOY, SETTER OF FIRES,
NOT TOO MUCH OUT OF THE ORDINARY

Dear Doctors:

Our Five-and-a-half-year-old son, Ralphie, is a fire setter. Ralphie is an outgoing, cheerful little boy who makes friends easily. He just instinctively says the right or cute thing. He tells Grandpa he loves him; tells Grandma her chicken pie is delicious. Actually, he gets on better with adults than with children because with children he likes to be the boss.

His interest in fire has been going on for about a year. He was playing with Daddy's cigarette lighter and hid in the closet and accidentally set fire to some clothes. In outdoor or indoor fireplaces he is always fooling around, throwing things in, poking at the fire.

We have let him toast marshmallows, etc., and even once tried the remedy you suggest of forcing him to light a whole box of kitchen matches, one at a time. He loved it! We have really tried everything, but he still sneaks matches whenever he can. Since I am a heavy smoker, we do have matches around. What can we try now?

We'd like to have him live long enough to grow up but if he keeps on with his interest in matches, we wonder.

Ralphie doesn't sound too out of the ordinary. Between Five and Six is one of the strongest fire-setting ages, and many little boys who have great difficulty in this department at this age do outgrow it nicely and grow up to be perfectly normal and well adjusted. When the fire setting continues on into Ten and Twelve, we feel that it has more adverse significance.

None of his fire-setting episodes sound unusual, much as you naturally dislike and even fear this kind of activity. Since you have tried the usual remedy of giving him acceptable, supervised experience with fire and it hasn't worked, we fear you are just going to have to supervise him a great deal more.

Clearly, you're going to have to keep all matches under lock and key. You might even have to give up smoking for a time. (Or use a lighter, which you keep in your pocket.) Some believe that fire setting in young children is a sign that something else is deeply wrong and the fire setting is just a symptom. This could be true in older children or, if very persistent, in younger ones. But with boys Ralphie's age their problem is mostly fascination with fire and a lack of self-restraint. So you have to supply the restraint by supervising; and Father will just have to step in with punishment when the supervising fails.

In some literary-minded children, reading books about fire (or being read to) can help absorb some of the fascination, but Ralphie does not sound too book-minded at this time. A visit to a fire station, which Four-year-olds so dearly love, might still be attractive to him. He might make friends with the firemen, and they might stand for the authority he needs.

DENTIST'S COOPERATION IS SUGGESTED
IN EFFORT TO STOP TONGUE SUCKING

Dear Doctors:

My problem is that my Five-year-old daughter, Agatha, sucks her tongue terribly, and almost constantly—when I comb her hair, or when she's playing quietly, and even at night, from the minute she hits the pillow and all during her sleep.

She sucks so loudly it has honestly awakened me in the next room.

I try to give her all the love and attention I can but I am a nervous, busy person. I had my children late in life.

Agatha was seven weeks premature, but now is healthy, happy, and good-natured. The tongue sucking didn't start until she was about Two-and-a-half.

Our doctor says just to ignore it, but that's hard to do as it's getting worse and her front teeth now seem to be protruding. She has very poor teeth with little enamel on them. The dentist gives her fluoride treatments.

I'm afraid her tongue sucking bothers the other children in school.

Since Agatha was premature, you should recalculate her age to be sure she really is ready for kindergarten. If she just made the age level, that is, if her birthday is for instance in September or earlier, you have to subtract the seven weeks prematurity. This would make her unready for school this year.

Thus, you wouldn't have to face the problem of tongue sucking in school for another year and it might possibly have gotten past its worst by then.

Since her teeth are so bad, we wonder if she doesn't need some medication such as calcium in addition to the help your dentist is giving her. Has your doctor considered giving any type of sedative?

With tongue sucking as with any tensional outlet, as you probably realize, we are interested more in calming the child down so that she doesn't need this outlet than simply in stopping the undesirable behavior.

Right now, at this young age and with the behavior so strongly entrenched, probably there is not too much you can do to attack it directly. But even in another year, say by summer, you might start planning with her, just as you do with the thumb sucker, that she will try to suck less.

You might discuss the problem with your dentist. He might become an influence in her life with relation to what the tongue sucking is doing to her teeth. In most cases we are against the wire devices (called rakes) that some dentists do put in children's mouths to prevent thumb sucking. But where the behavior is so extreme and definitely damaging to her (already poor) teeth, you might want to consider even such an extreme measure.

IS IT BAD FOR A FIVE-YEAR-OLD TO SAY
"I HATE YOU"?

Dear Doctors:

I don't want to be a fussy grandmother or a critical mother-in-law, but some things are just too much.

Just recently I took my daughter-in-law and my two little grandchildren, Frank, aged Five-and-a-half, and Frannie, just Three, to the zoo. Admittedly, it was rather a long afternoon.

And the zoo we visited seemed to have the animals up in their cages, quite a distance from the viewers. So the whole thing may have been somewhat of a disappointment to the children.

Perhaps predictably, it wasn't long before Frank

wanted something to eat. And then he wanted a balloon. Both these wishes were granted.

Finally we got into the car to go home and Frank started fussing for a drink. Well, we didn't have anything to drink in the car and his mother told him so.

He went into a real tantrum and after saying several very unpleasant things (which would never have been allowed in my own children), he yelled, "I wish we hadn't gone to the zoo. I hate everybody in this car!"

To my amazement, his mother ignored this whole outburst. Believe me, any child of mine who spoke that way would have gotten a good sound spanking right on the spot. And I told my daughter-in-law so. Don't you think I was right?

Well, actually, no. Shouting "I hate you" for a Five- to Six-year-old is a lot like having a temper tantrum for a preschooler. Both types of behavior tell us things have just gone too far and the child is exploding in the only way that he or she knows.

Nobody likes to be told "I hate you," but when it is said by the very young child it usually means little more than "I'm unhappy, sad, mixed up, tired, frustrated, and I'm going to take it out on anybody or everybody in sight."

As a rule it does not mean "I have thought things over carefully and I really do hate you."

I think your daughter-in-law did right to ignore her son's outburst. The chances are that the whole zoo trip was a little too long and too demanding for a Five-and-a-half-year-old, let alone for a Three-year-old.

The path of wisdom might be to keep all excursions short and not too frequent.

And whatever the problem—serious or simple—it is really up to Mother and Father and not Grandmother to decide how children should be disciplined.

EPILOGUE

This perhaps should come as a prologue rather than an epilogue, because we would like to alert every parent in advance that Five may be one of the nicest ages you will ever encounter. Your time with your Five-year-old may well be one of the most rewarding periods in your entire relationship with your son or daughter.

What is so glorious about the typical Five-year-old is that to Five, *you,* the care-giving parent, are the center of the universe. He or she wants to please you, wants to be good, wants to do right.

This pinnacle of affirmation, this peak of perfection, may in all likelihood be never met with again. So enjoy it while it lasts. Don't spoil it, as some parents have been known to do, by worrying that your child may be "almost too good." Few things last forever, and the charming docility and desire to please, so characteristic of the typical Five-year-old, all too soon gives way to the more tangled complexity so predictably characteristic of Six.

APPENDIXES
Good Toys
for Five-Year-Olds

For the Five-year-old, the most enjoyable play may involve other children and a clear relationship with the real world. But he still likes some of the Four-year-old kinds of toys that use energy and direct it in constructive ways.[9]

Beads
Blocks
Board games, simple
Cameras, simple
    (Instamatic)
Card games, simple
Cooking equipment
Crafts involving
    small-muscle coordina-
    tion (loop looms, spool
    knitting, simple sewing)
Crayons
Doctor kits
Dollhouses with furniture
Dolls with many
    accessories
Drawing materials
Dress-up materials for
    particular occupations

(nurse, policeman,
    astronaut, fireman,
    doctor, carpenter)
Fingerpaints
Flashlight
Housekeeping equipment
    of all kinds
Ice skates
Jigsaw puzzles
Jump rope
Kites
Miniature forts, filling
    stations, farms
Miniature people, animals,
    vehicles
Modeling materials that
    dry or bake to a
    permanent finish
Paints

Phonograph records
Picture lotto
Poster paints
Punching bag
Puzzles
Roller skates
Science materials (magnets, magnifying glass, stethoscope)
Scooter
Skipping rope
Stilts
Toy soldiers
Trains
Tricycle
Wheel toys of all kinds: trucks, bulldozers, tractors, trains
Workbench with saw, vise, screwdriver, wrench

Books for
Five-Year-Olds

Adler, David. *A Little At a Time.* New York: Random House, 1976.

Benton, Robert. *Don't Ever Wish for a Seven-Foot Bear.* New York: Knopf, 1972.

Bloome, Enid. *Dogs Don't Belong on Beds.* New York: Doubleday, 1974.

Boden, Alice. *The Field of Buttercups.* New York: Walck, 1974.

Borack, Barbara. *Gooney.* New York: Harper & Row, 1975.

Brinkloe, Julie. *The Spider Web.* New York: Scribner, 1975.

Brown, Margaret Wise. *Three Little Animals,* New York: Harper & Row, 1965.

———. *Fox Eyes.* New York: Pantheon, 1977.

———. *The Runaway Bunny* (paperback). New York: Harper & Row, 1977.

Duvoisin, Roger. *The Rain Puddle.* New York: Lothrop, Lee & Shepard, 1965.

———. *Jasmine.* New York: Knopf, 1973.

———. *The Crocodile in the Tree.* New York: Knopf, 1973.

———. *Petunia's Treasure.* New York: Knopf, 1975.

———. *Crocus.* New York: Knopf, 1977.

Emberly, Ed. *Klippity Klop.* Boston: Little, Brown, 1974.

Ernst, Kathryn. *Danny and His Thumb.* Englewood Cliffs, N.J.: Prentice-Hall, 1972.

Farber, Norma. *As I Was Crossing Boston Common.* New York: Dutton, 1975.

French, Fiona. *King Tree.* New York: Walck, 1973.

Garland, Sarah. *The Joss Bird.* New York: Scribner, 1975.

Hafter, Richard. *Colors.* New York: A Strawberry Book, Larousse & Co., 1975.

———. *Yes and No: A Book of Opposites.* New York: A Strawberry Book, Larousse & Co., 1975.

Hoban, Russell. *Bedtime for Frances.* New York: Harper & Row, 1960.

———, and Selig, Sylvia. *Ten What? A Mystery Counting Book.* New York: Scribner, 1975.

Jewett, Nancy. *Cheer Up Pig.* New York: Harper & Row, 1975.

Kahn, Joan. *You Can't Catch Me.* New York: Harper & Row, 1976.

Kessler, Ethel. *Do Baby Bears Sit on Chairs?* Garden City, N.Y.: Doubleday, 1961.

Kraus, Robert. *The Little Giant.* New York: Windmill/Dutton, 1977.

Kuskin, Karla. *Roar and More* (paperback). New York: Harper & Row, 1977.

Lionni, Leo. *Swimmy.* New York: Pantheon, 1963.

———. *A Color of His Own.* New York: Pantheon, 1975.

Manushkin, Fran. *Shirley Bird.* New York: Harper & Row, 1975.

Miller, Edna. *Mousekins Woodland Sleepers.* Englewood Cliffs, N.J.: Prentice-Hall, 1974.

Moffett, Martha. *A Flower Pot Is Not a Hat.* New York: Dutton, 1972.

Petie, Harriet. *Billions of Bugs.* Englewood Cliffs, N.J.: Prentice-Hall, 1975.

Pinkwater, Daniel. *The Blue Thing.* Englewood Cliffs, N.J.: Prentice-Hall, 1977.

Richelson, Geraldine. *What Is a Child?* New York: A Harlan Quist Book, n.d.

———. *What Is a Grownup?* New York: A Harlan Quist Book, n.d.

Sazer, Nina. *What Do You Think I Saw?* New York: Pantheon, 1976.

Schulevitz, Uri. *Dawn.* New York: Farrar, Straus & Giroux, 1974.

Silverstein, Shel. *The Giving Tree.* New York: Harper & Row, 1964.

Stein, Sara Bonnett. *Making Babies.* New York: Walker, 1974.

————. *That New Baby.* New York: Walker, 1974.

Thompson, Jean. *I'm Going to Run Away.* New York: Abingdon Press, 1975.

Ungerer, Toni. *The Beast of Mr. Racine.* New York: Farrar, Straus & Giroux, 1971.

————. *Crictor.* New York: Harper & Row, 1958.

Watson, Sitzer; and Hirschberg. *Just Look At Me Now.* New York: Golden Book, 1977.

Williams, Barbara. *Some Day Said Michael.* New York: Dutton, 1976.

Williams, Margery. *The Velveteen Rabbit.* Garden City, N.Y.: Doubleday, n.d.

Zindel, Paul. *I Love My Mother.* New York: Harper & Row, 1975.

Zolotow, Charlotte. *Hold My Hand.* New York: Harper & Row, 1973.

Books for the Parents of Five-Year-Olds

Ames, Louise Bates. *Parents Ask.* A syndicated daily newspaper column. New Haven, Conn: Gesell Institute, 1952–.
———. *Child Care and Development.* Philadelphia: Lippincott, rev. ed., 1978.
———. *Is Your Child in the Wrong Grade?* New York: Harper & Row, 1967.
———, and Chase, Joan Ames. *Don't Push Your Preschooler.* New York: Harper & Row, 1974.
———, and Ilg, Frances L. *Your Four-Year-Old: Wild and Wonderful.* New York: Delacorte, 1976.
Austin, John J., and Lafferty, J. Clayton. *Ready or Not? The School Readiness Checklist.* Muskegon, Mich.: Research Concepts, 1963.
Beekman, Daniel. *The Mechanical Baby: A Popular History of the Theory and Practice of Child Raising.* New York: Lawrence Hill & Co., 1977.
Benning, Lee. *How to Bring Up a Child Without Spending a Fortune.* New York: McKay, 1975.
Braga, Laurie, and Braga, Joseph. *Learning and Growing: A Guide to Child Development.* Englewood Cliffs, N.J.: Prentice-Hall, 1975.
Brazleton, T. Berry. *Doctor and Child.* New York: Delacorte, 1976.

Briggs, Dorothy Corkille. *Your Child's Self-Esteem.* New York: Doubleday, 1970.

Caplan, Frank, and Caplan, Theresa. *The Power of Play.* New York: Doubleday, 1973.

Coffin, Patricia. *1, 2, 3, 4, 5, 6. How to Understand and Enjoy the Years That Count.* New York: Macmillan, 1972.

Collier, Herbert. *The Psychology of Twins: A Practical Handbook.* Phoenix, Ariz.: Twins (P.O. Box 155606, Phoenix, Arizona), 1972.

Comer, James P., and Pouissant, Alvin F. *Black Child Care: How to Bring Up a Healthy Black Child in America.* New York: Simon & Schuster, 1975.

DeRosis, Helen. *Parent Power Child Power.* New York: McGraw-Hill, 1975.

Dodson, Fitzhugh. *How to Parent.* Los Angeles: Nash, 1970.

———. *How to Father.* Los Angeles: Nash, 1974.

———. *How to Discipline with Love.* New York: Rawson, 1977.

Feingold, Ben J. *Why Your Child Is Hyperactive.* New York: Random House, 1975.

Forer, Lucille K. *The Birth Order Factor.* New York: McKay, 1976.

Gardner, Richard A. *Understanding Children.* New York: Aronson, 1973.

———. *The Parents' Book About Divorce.* New York: Doubleday, 1977.

Gesell, Arnold, et al. *The First Five Years of Life.* New York: Harper & Row, 1940.

———; Ilg, Frances L.; and Ames, Louise Bates. *The Child From Five to Ten.* New York: Harper & Row, rev. ed., 1974.

Grollman, Earl A., ed. *Explaining Death to Children.* Boston: Beacon Press, 1967.

———. *Explaining Divorce to Children.* Boston: Beacon Press, 1969.

Harrison-Ross, Phyllis, and Wyden, Barbara. *The Black Child: A Parent's Guide.* New York: Peter Wyden, 1973.

• *Appendixes* •

Hautzig, Esther. *Life With Working Parents.* New York: Macmillan, 1977.

Hedges, William D. *At What Age Should Children Enter First Grade: A Comprehensive Review of the Research.* Ann Arbor, Mich.: University Microfilms International (300 North Zeeb Road), 1977.

Ilg, Frances L.; Ames, Louise Bates; Gillespie, Clyde; and Haines, Jacqueline. *School Readiness.* New York: Harper & Row, rev., 1978.

Jones, Hettie. *How to Eat Your ABC'S: A Book About Vitamins.* New York: Four Winds Press, 1976.

LeShan, Eda. *How to Survive Parenthood.* New York: Random House, 1965.

————. *Learning to Say Goodbye: When A Parent Dies.* New York: Macmillan, 1976.

Levine, Milton, and Seligmann, Jean. *The Parents' Encyclopedia of Infancy, Childhood and Adolescence.* New York: Crowell, 1973.

Liepmann, Lise. *Your Child's Sensory World.* New York: Dial, 1973.

McIntire, Roger W. *For Love of Children.* Del Mar, Calif.: CRM Books, 1970.

Maynard, Fredelle. *Guiding Your Child to a More Creative Life.* New York: Doubleday, 1973. (Contains excellent lists of books for parents on arts and crafts, drawing, painting, crayoning, clay modeling, ceramics, fabrics and yarns, puppets, and children's records.)

Pantell, Robert H.; Fries, James F.; and Vickery, Donald M. *Taking Care of Your Child: A Parents' Guide to Medical Care.* New York: Addison-Wesley, 1977.

Peck, Ellen. *The Joy of the Only Child.* New York: Delacorte, 1977.

Schiff, Harriet Sarnoff. *The Bereaved Parent.* New York: Crown, 1977.

Sheldon, William H. *Varieties of Temperament.* New York: Hafner, 1970.

Smith, Lendon. *Improving Your Child's Behavior Chemistry.* Englewood Cliffs, N.J.: Prentice-Hall, 1976.

Thomas, Alexander, and Chess, Stella. *Temperament and Development.* New York: Brunner/Mazel, 1977.

Warner, Silas, and Rosenberg, Edward B. *Your Child Learns Naturally.* New York: Doubleday, 1977.

Wunderlich, Ray. *Allergy, Brains and Children Coping.* St. Petersburg, Fla.: Johnny Reads Press, 1973.

Young, Milton A. *Buttons Are to Push: Developing Your Child's Creativity.* New York: Pitman, 1970.

NOTES

1. Feingold, Ben. *Why Your Child Is Hyperactive* (New York: Random House, 1975).
2. Wunderlich, Ray C. *Allergy, Brains and Children Coping* (St. Petersburg, Fla.: Johnny Reads Press, 1973).
3. Smith, Lendon J. *Improving Your Child's Behavior Chemistry* (Englewood Cliffs, N.J.: Prentice-Hall, 1976).
4. Ames, Louis Bates. *Is Your Child in the Wrong Grade?* (New York: Harper & Row, 1967). Ames, Louise Bates; Ilg, Frances L.; Haines, Jacqueline; and Gillespie, Clyde. *School Readiness* (New York: Harper & Row, rev., 1978).
5. Hedges, William D. *At What Age Should Children Enter First Grade: A Comprehensive Review of the Research* (Ann Arbor, Mich.: University Microfilms International, 1977).
6. Austin, John J., and Lafferty, Clayton J. *Ready or Not? The School Readiness Checklist* (Muskegon, Mich.: Research Concepts, 1963).
7. From *Handbook for Prekindergarten and Kindergarten Teachers* (Cheshire Public Schools, Cheshire, Conn.) (Dr. Stephen August, Superintendent.) Published in 1968 through courtesy of ACES.
8. Chess, Stella, and Thomas, Alexander. "Temperamen-

tal Traits and Parental Guidance," Chapter 12 in *Helping Parents Help Their Children,* ed. by L. Eugene Arnold (New York: Brunner/Mazel, 1978).

9. The reader is especially referred to Fredelle Maynard's *Guiding Your Child to a More Creative Life* (New York: Doubleday, 1973), for very full detail on the child's play life.

INDEX

• *Index* •